D1707501

BUILDING
THE VICTORY

The Order Book
of the
Volunteer Engineer Brigade,
Army of the Potomac
October 1863–May 1865

Edited by Philip Katcher

 White Mane Books

This White Mane Books publication
was printed by

Beidel Printing House, Inc.
63 West Burd Street
Shippensburg, PA 17257-0152 USA

In respect for the scholarship contained herein, the acid-free paper used in this book meets the guidelines for permanence and durability of the Committee on Production Guidelines for Book Longevity of the Council on Library Resources.

For a complete list of available publications please write

White Mane Books
Division of White Mane Publishing Company, Inc.
P.O. Box 152
Shippensburg, PA 17257-0152 USA

Library of Congress Cataloging-in-Publication Data

Building the victory : the order book of the Volunteer Engineer
    Brigade, Army of the Potomac, October 1863-May 1865 / edited by
    Philip Katcher.
        p.   cm.
    Includes bibliographical references (p.   ) and index.
    ISBN 1-57249-080-2 (alk. paper)
    1. United States. Army. Volunteer Engineer Brigade (1862-1865)
    2. United States--History--Civil War, 1861-1865--Regimental
    histories--Sources. 3. United States--History--Civil War,
    1861-1865--Engineering and construction--Sources. 4. United States.
    Army--Order-books. I. Katcher, Philip R. N. II. United States.
    Army. Volunteer Engineer Brigade (1862-1865)
    E493.5.V65B85   1998
    973.7' 4--dc21   97-52210
                                                        CIP

PRINTED IN THE UNITED STATES OF AMERICA

Table of Contents

Introduction

◀━━━━━━━━━━━━▶

If it was the infantry who bore the brunt of Civil War combat, it was the engineers who got them to where they could fight. Engineers built roads and bridges that allowed the troops to move forward and their supplies to reach the front. It was not a heroic job, but it was an extremely vital one.

The Union's Army of the Potomac, that force gathered around Washington early in the war to take Richmond, capital of the Confederacy, was at first served by the regular U.S. Army's battalion of engineers. However, this proved too small a force to do all the building of works necessary to support well over 100,000 men in the field. Two volunteer engineer regiments from New York were organized and placed into what became the Volunteer Engineer Brigade.

Although engineers were important in every one of the army's campaigns, especially the 1862 Peninsula Campaign, they were most important in the last campaign of the war. In 1864 Lieutenant General U.S. Grant arrived from the west determined to drive the eastern army unstoppingly until the Confederate army facing them was destroyed. This would take constant marching, bridge building, and road laying. Engineers would work as never before. The last years of the war were, therefore, the busiest and most important of all to the volunteer engineers.

While professionals, the engineers were also members of a military organization. They had to be drilled in the elaborate infantry drill of the period. Men disobeyed orders and had to be punished. Men were switched from job to job. Men went on furlough. And for each one of these deeds, an order had to be recorded by a clerk in headquarters. These orders were placed into the brigade order book.

The order book of a unit, be it a company or a brigade, is the heart of that organization. Maintained by clerks in the adjutant's office, it contains the details involved in the unit's day-to-day life. It explains who does what

v

and who did what. It explains what should be done in the future and, as it does, what had been done or left undone in the past.

This book is based on the previously unpublished order book of the Volunteer Engineer Brigade from late 1863 until the brigade was mustered out in early 1865. It has been augmented with explanations of what specific orders mean, as well as with an indication of the activities of brigade member units at the times. It contains special orders, orders that pertain to individuals only, and general orders which pertain to the entire brigade. Many of the orders are written in abbreviations that would have been known to virtually everyone in the military; I have retained these novel spellings and abbreviations, as well as the original punctuation, spelling, and capitalization.

Special thanks is due to Vicki Betts of Texas who directed me to available sources on the brigade.

CHAPTER 1
Three Years of War

◄──────────────►

In the modern U.S. Army there are four, not just three, branches of the service considered "combat arms." These include the expected infantry, artillery, and cavalry, but as well include one which might not be considered a combat arm, the Corps of Engineers. So it was in the Civil War, too, the Corps of Engineers was both a support and a combat arm.

According to the standard military reference of the Civil War period, Scott's *Military Dictionary*, the engineers had one of the largest assignments of any branch of service: "The engineers are charged with planning, constructing, and repairing all fortifications and other defensive works; with disbursements of money connected with these operations. In time of war, they present plans for the attack and defence of military works; lay out and construct field defences, redoubts, intrenchments, roads, &c.; form a part of the vanguard to remove obstructions; and in retreat, form a part of the rear guard, to erect obstacles, destroy roads, bridges, &c., so as to retard an enemy's pursuit."[1]

The Corps is one of the oldest branches of service in the U.S. Army, having been authorized by Congress on March 11, 1779. It had been disbanded along with the bulk of the Continental Army in November 1783, but it was soon apparent that a growing country with a large frontier needed trained military engineers, and the Corps was again authorized May 9, 1794.

At the same time, Congress decided that the functions of the Corps should not include map making, and authorized the hiring of a "geographer and surveyor of the roads" on July 25, 1777. On March 3, 1813, however, during the country's second war with Britain, Congress set up an establishment of topographical engineers, which, in August 1818, became the Corps of Topographical Engineers. According to Scott's *Military Dictionary*, "The duties of the corps consist in surveys for the defence of the frontiers, and of positions for fortifications, in reconnoissances of the country through which an army has to pass, or in which it has to operate; in the examination of all routes of communications by land or by water, both for supplies and military movements; in the construction of military roads and permanent bridges connected with them; and the charge of the construction of all civil works, authorized by acts of Congress, not specially assigned by law to some other branch of the service."[2]

Most of the men in these two branches of engineers were officers. Indeed, they were officers who were set apart from the rest of the army. "The officers of Engineers are not to assume nor to be ordered on any duty beyond the line of their immediate profession, except by the special order of the President," according to Army Regulations. "Officers of the corps of Engineers...though eligible to command according to the rank they hold in the army of the United States, shall not assume the command of troops unless put on duty under orders which specially so direct by authority of the President."[3]

At the outbreak of the Civil War the U.S. Army had only one company of enlisted men, known as Sappers, Miners, & Pontoniers, in its Corps of Engineers. The bulk of the Corps was made up of officers assigned to staffs of generals or at posts to supervise the building of fortifications. The men who actually built the fortifications were hired civilian laborers. The jobs of the pontoniers, sappers, and miners were the traditional jobs of military engineers. Pontoniers lay pontoon bridges, built across boats made of wood, or plain- or rubber-coated canvas, across bodies of water. Sappers dug trenches and built field fortifications. Miners dug mines and countermines during sieges.

Recalled one Union artilleryman who saw service in Virginia later: "The engineers' special duties were to make roads passable for the army by corduroying sloughs, building trestle bridges across small streams, laying pontoon bridges over rivers, and taking up the same, laying out and building fortifications, and slashing."[4]

A single company of trained enlisted engineers was considered more than enough for the pre-war army. Indeed, Winfield Scott had only one company of Sappers, Miners, & Pontoniers in his army that took Mexico City in 1848. But it was soon recognized that it would take a lot more trained military engineers to aid in putting down rebellion in the South. On August 3, 1861, Congress authorized six more lieutenants in both engineers and topographical engineers, as well as three more companies of enlisted engineers, "and each of the four companies of engineer soldiers shall hereafter be composed of ten sergeants, ten corporals, two musicians, sixty-four privates of the first class, or artificers, and sixty-four privates of the second class; in all, one hundred and fifty men each."[5] A company of enlisted men was added to the Corps of Topographical Engineers, along with two more lieutenant colonels and four more majors, on August 6, 1861. "The said company shall be subject to the Rules and Articles of War, and shall have the same organization as the companies of engineer soldiers attached to the Corps of Engineers."[6]

These companies in the Corps of Engineers made up, with the pre-war company, the U.S. Engineer Battalion. The battalion's four companies were based in Washington, where they had been trained for such tasks as building pontoon bridges and field fortifications under fire where civilian laborers, obviously, could not be trusted. The problem was that, despite a number of recruiting booths the Corps opened across the country, the entire Corps of Engineers consisted of only 276 enlisted men by July 1, 1862. There was, however, no authorization for volunteer units to be raised as engineers; indeed, the volunteer militia that the nation depended on for its defense was virtually all infantry, with a smattering of cavalry and artillery, which were rather more expensive organizations to equip.

Some individuals, however, saw that the size of armies that would be needed to subdue the South would require more enlisted engineers than one battalion. In October 1861 Edward Serrell began organizing an all-volunteer regiment, the 1st Regiment of New York Volunteer Engineers, in New York City. As well, a 2nd New York Engineer Regiment was authorized. Recruiting was, however, slow, as many men sought the glory of the bayonet charge instead of the tedium of hammering nails to save the Union. The 1st New York was taken along on an expedition down the southern Atlantic coast, with some companies leaving as early as October 1861, while would-be officers of the 2nd New York Engineers tried to drum up men for their companies in New York.

Even with these organizations accepted into Federal service, it would not be until July 17, 1862, that Congress recognized the volunteer engineers officially. On that date it passed a law stating that

> the different regiments and independent companies heretofore mustered into the service of the United States as volunteer engineers, pioneers, or sappers and miners, under the orders of the President or Secretary of War, or by authority of the commanding general of any military department of the United States, or which, having been mustered into the service as infantry, shall be reorganized, and employed as engineers, pioneers, or sappers and miners, shall be, and the same are hereby, recognized and accepted as volunteer engineers, on the same footing, in all respects, in regard to their organization, pay, and emoluments, as the Corps of Engineers of the Regular Army of the United States, and they shall be paid for their services, already performed, as is now provided by law for the payment of officers, noncommissioned officers, and privates of the Engineer Corps of the Regular Army.[7]

Such pay was higher than for the same ranks in other branches of the service. Engineer colonels received $110 a month; lieutenant colonels, $95; majors, $80; captains, $70; and first and second lieutenants, $53.33. Engineer sergeants received $34 a month, compared to $17 a month paid to infantry sergeants. Engineer corporals received $20 a month; artificers, $17; second class privates, $13; and musicians, $12.

Neither the 1st nor the 2d New York Volunteer Regiments joined the force around Washington which was being turned into the Union's main eastern theater front-line army. This army, soon named the Army of the Potomac, was to have what many at the time considered the most important job for Union troops in the war, the capture of the capital of the Confederacy, Richmond. Richmond had been earmarked as a major target from the very beginning. It held not only the seat of the South's new government, but it was the largest industrial city in a mostly agrarian South. Its Tredegar Iron Works was the only industrial plant in the South that could roll armor plate for warships and iron rails for railroads. Its woolen mills were eventually to produce most of the cloth used in the army defending the city, the Army of Northern Virginia.

The two regiments of volunteer engineers were not sent south with the first attempt to take Richmond, under Major General Irwin McDowell. This attempt ended in the fiasco of the First Bull Run, which saw many Union soldiers break under fire and not stop their informal retreats until they reached the Long Bridge across the Potomac into Washington, out of the feared Commonwealth of Virginia.

After that bungled invasion, President Abraham Lincoln gave command of the army to an officer of the pre-war Corps of Engineers, Major General of Volunteers George B. McClellan. A serious student of war, McClellan, who had acquired a fine record as an officer of the Corps of Topographical Engineers during the Mexican War, settled down to mold the untrained volunteers into a professional military force.

McClellan saw that the handful of Regular Army enlisted engineers would be insufficient for his needs, based on his past experience as well as a knowledge of the river-torn area through which he must march. "The number of engineer troops being entirely inadequate to the necessities of the army," McClellan reported later, "an effort was made to partially remedy this defect by detailing the Fifteenth and Fiftieth New York Volunteers, which contained many sailors and mechanics, as engineer troops. They were first placed under the immediate superintendence of Lieut. Col. B.S. Alexander, U.S. Engineers, by whom they were instructed in the duties of pontoniers, and became somewhat familiar with those of sappers and miners."[8]

Alexander, who had been born in Kentucky in 1819 and graduated from the U.S. Military Academy in 1842 seventh in his class, had gone directly into the Corps of Engineers. He had been in charge of a number of building projects in Massachusetts and New York at West Point before the war. He began the war as a staff engineer in one of McDowell's divisions, seeing service at the 1st Bull Run. By then, he had a temporary rank of lieutenant colonel, although he was still listed as a captain of engineers on the official army register. On April 1, 1862, he was assigned the task of instructing engineering troops for the Army of the Potomac, largely the new volunteer engineers.

As well, qualified men were recruited from the beginning to serve as engineers. Captain Wesley Brainerd, one of the early company commanders in the volunteer New York organizations, issued a poster designed to attract mechanics, carpenters, farmers, and ordinary laborers to his company of engineers. The attraction, he said, was that "This Engineer Regiment is to be one of the best in the service, and as the principal duties in this Corps will be of a professional character a position in it is more desirable than of equal rank in ordinary Infantry Regiments."[9]

On October 25, 1861, McClellan had the 15th Regiment of New York Volunteer Engineers created in Washington by turning the men who had enlisted into the 15th New York Infantry into engineers. The regiment had been raised as an infantry regiment in New York City, being mustered in there for two years' service on June 17, 1861. They had been equipped with M1853, 0.577 caliber British-made rifled muskets, as had the men of the 1st New York Engineers. A dozen days later the regiment was sent on to Washington, where it had served in the city's garrison. The regiment, commanded by Colonel John McLeod Murphy, helped build Fort Ward, one of the main posts in the chain of forts around Washington for that city's defense. Its construction began in September 1861, although work on improving the fort would last until its need was long gone, in May 1865.

On October 22, the would-be infantrymen of the 50th New York found themselves turning in their novel gray uniforms trimmed with green cord for regulation blue coats trimmed in yellow for the Engineer Corps as members of the new 50th New York Volunteer Engineer Regiment. The 50th had been raised in Elmira, New York, being formally organized there on September 18. It had been in Washington since September 22, posted largely around the Navy Yard, not far from the place that would become the Engineer Depot. Colonel Charles B. Stuart commanded the 50th, which was armed with M1854 Austrian 0.54 caliber rifled muskets.

This move probably pleased many lieutenants who would have had to have walked everywhere their companies went in the infantry. Wrote one lieutenant of the 15th home, "Let me say that all commissioned [officers] of the Engineer Corps have to be mounted. It is the highest branch of service. The pay is better and their duty requires them to be mounted."[10]

Training began for the officers, who were then to train noncommissioned officers and men. They worked from a number of manuals in class rooms prior to taking the field. The most important of these manuals had been written by a professor at the U.S. Military Academy, D.H. Mahan, back in 1836, but had been reprinted in 1861 for the use of these new military engineers. *A Treatise on Field Fortifications*, as it was titled, also was reprinted in 1863. As well, Mahan produced *An Elementary Course in Civil Engineering for the Use of Cadets in the United States Military Academy* which had been published in 1857 and was still available. Captain T.J. Lee of the Corps of Topographical Engineers published his *Tables and Formulae* in 1853, and this book, too, was still available. Captain James C. Duane, who would serve as chief engineer in the Army of the Potomac, published his *Manual for Engineer Troops* in 1861. This book, which would be often reprinted during the war, covered building pontoon bridges, conducting a siege, the "school of the sap," military mining, and the construction of batteries.

On October 31 the War Department set up the organization of these new units. Each regiment was to contain a colonel, a lieutenant-colonel, three majors, an adjutant who ranked as a lieutenant and was to be taken from one of the companies as was the quartermaster, a chaplain, a surgeon who ranked as a major, two assistant surgeons who ranked as captains, a hospital steward who was an enlisted man with some medical training who held a senior noncommissioned officer's grade, three quartermaster sergeants, and three commissary sergeants. Each company included a captain, two first lieutenants, a second lieutenant, two musicians who were generally drummers, although one was sometimes a fifer, ten sergeants, ten corporals, 64 artificers or privates of the first class, and 64 privates of the second class.[11]

McClellan placed Captain Duane, a professional soldier from the Corps of Engineers, in charge of organizing the army's first pontoon train. McClellan, who had spent time in Europe as part of an official group of military observers to study European armies in action, ordered Duane to have pontoon bridges built that were copies of the latest French model, as McClellan felt that the older U.S. style, based on a rubber-coated canvas boat, was "entirely useless for the general purposes of a campaign."[12]

Laying these pontoon bridges took some training and practice. The bridges were carried on a train that included 34 pontoon wagons, 17 chess wagons, abutment wagons, traveling forges, and tool wagons. The abutment wagons carried one of the most important parts of the bridging equipment, the abutment still. This was a 16-foot-long beam backed by a board that rose four inches above it. That four inches was the dimension of the balks, the beams that connected the pontoons to make the bays. Flooring boards, called chesses, were laid across from balk to balk.

A member of Company A, U.S. Engineers described the process of bridge building with this equipment:

Four or five with spades and other implements improvised a wooden abutment on the shore; another party rowed against the stream, moored a scow, and let it drift down until it was opposite the wooden abutment; then a part of ten advanced, each two men carrying a claw-balk, or timbers fitted with a claw, one of which held the gunwale of the boat, the other the shore abutment. Twenty men now came down on the left with planks [called chesses], one inch thick, six inches wide, and fifteen feet long, narrowed at each end; these they laid across the five joists or balks, and returned on the right.

Another party meanwhile moored another boat, which dropped down-stream opposite the one already bridged; five joists, each twenty feet long, were laid upon the gunwale five men; these were fastened by those in the boat, by means of ropes, to cleats or hooks provided for the purpose on the side of the scows, which were shoved off from the shore until the shore end of the balk rested upon the shore boat. These were covered with planks in the same manner as before; side-rails of joists were lashed down with ropes to secure the whole. So one after another of the boats was dropped into position until a bridge several hundred feet long reached from the Maryland to the Virginia shore, for the passage of artillery and every description of munitions for an army.

Owing to the force of the current, a large rope cable was stretched from shore to shore fifty feet above the bridge, and the upper end of each boat was stayed to the cable by a smaller rope.[13]

Once the bridge was built, it was put into quick use. Then, when the rest of the army had crossed over it, it had to be taken apart and repacked on wagons. Wrote a correspondent with the Army of the Potomac:

When an army had crossed a pontoon-bridge and pressed on in pursuit of the enemy, the bridge would be taken apart, the boats and the tackle loaded on to the wagons, and the pontoon-train would in a few hours reach the head of the column again, in full readiness to facilitate further advance of the army. At times a railroad-bridge would be destroyed by the enemy's rear guard and the engineers would obtain a duplicate bridge from the rear and quickly get it into place.[14]

As well, the Army of the Potomac's engineers spent much time preparing roads. In this they were aided by infantrymen drawn from nearby units, since making roads passable was a labor-intensive activity. One artilleryman later recalled:

Corduroying called at times for a large amount of labor, for Virginia mud was such a foe to rapid transit that miles upon miles of this sort of road had to be laid to keep ready communication between different portions of the army. Where the ground was miry, two stringers were laid longitudinally of the ground, and on these the corduroy of logs, averaging, perhaps, four inches in diameter was laid, and a cover of brush was sometimes spread upon it to prevent mules from thrusting their lags through. Where the surface was simply muddy, no stringers were used.[15]

As well, engineers had to be trained in the special devices used in fortifications. Their use began with laying out the lines to be fortified. Recalled Edwin Forbes, an artist and correspondent who accompanied the Army of the Potomac:

> The Engineer Corps was often called upon to lay out a line of breastworks to cover the front of the army from a surprise. It is not easy to realize how severe this labor was and how hard the soldiers worked at it. A ditch had first to be dug in the front with pick and spade; then the trees were felled by the axe, cut into lengths, and used as a backing for the bank of earth thrown up from the ditch. Traverses were built to protect men and guns from flanking fire, and the front covered by an abatis made of limbs of trees lying lengthwise with sharpened ends placed toward the enemy. Another fence which is sometimes placed in front of a fortified line is made by sharpening heavy logs and burying butts in the ground with points forward. This can be removed only by the axe, and if attempted under fire great loss of life is the result.[16]

Then they had to assemble the special devices used in making the fortifications secure from attack. These, recalled the artilleryman, included:

> The *Gabions*, being hollow cylinders of wicker-work without bottom filled with earth, and placed on the earthworks; the *Fascines*, being bundles of small sticks bound at both ends and intermediate points, to aid in raising batteries, filling ditches, etc.; *Chevaux-de-fris* [sic], a piece of timber traversed with wooded spikes, used especially as a defence against cavalry; the *Abatis*, a row of the large branches of trees, sharpened and laid close together, points outward, with the bottoms pinned to the ground; the *Fraise*, a defence of pointed sticks, fastened into the ground at such an incline as to bring the points breast-high:—all these were fashioned by the engineer corps, in vast numbers, when the army was besieging Petersburg in 1864.[17]

The ground before the fortifications had to be cleared so the defenders would have fields of fire that covered the area in front of them. Wrote the artilleryman:

> When a line of works was laid out through woods, much slashing, or felling of trees, was necessary in its front. This was especially necessary in front of forts and batteries. Much of this labor was done by the engineers. The trees were felled with their tops toward the enemy, leaving stumps about three feet high. The territory covered by these fallen trees was called the Slashes, hence Slashing. No large body of the enemy could safely attempt a passage through such an obstacle. It was a strong defence for a weak line of works.[18]

Training went on for months as summer turned into fall. The last of the dried leaves blew from parade grounds, and snow covered the tented fields around Washington as the officers and men drilled on. The snows melted. Still the army remained in its winter quarters. Needed supplies were stockpiled for an eventual advance. Among engineer equipment, McClellan wrote, was enough equipment for bridge building, "consisting of bateaux with the anchors and flooring material (French model) trestles, and engineer's tools, with the necessary wagons for their transportation."[19]

Infantry drill was also stressed for the engineers. Their dress parades grew sharper and finer. But, Lincoln felt, the purpose of this army was not to show itself off in elaborate but safe maneuvers—it was to find and destroy the Confederate army in Virginia, to take the Richmond, and to overthrow its government to restore Federal rule. He began to nag more and more at McClellan to move, even issuing general orders calling for all Federal forces to move on Washington's Birthday.

McClellan did not move.

What McClellan did do, however, was prepare a plan that called for a seaborne movement from Washington, to the east of Richmond along the peninsula of land between the James and Rappahannock Rivers. Lincoln approved the plan with some misgivings, seeing a great deal of open, undefended ground between the Confederate army and Washington's line of forts with McClellan's Army of the Potomac no longer between the two capital cities.

But, finally, McClellan did move, and the two regiments of New York Engineers with him. They were placed into the Volunteer Engineer Brigade, then under the command of Brigadier General Daniel Phineas Woodbury, Alexander staying to supervise construction in the defenses of Washington. Woodbury was 49 years old at the time, a New Hampshire native who had studied at Dartmouth College before entering the U.S. Military Academy in 1832. On being graduated four years later, he was assigned to the artillery, but soon thereafter was transferred to the Corps of Engineers. Most of his military career had been spent in construction projects, including Forts Taylor, Jefferson, Kearny, Laramie, and Warren in various parts of the country, and the Cumberland Road in Ohio. By 1853 he had married into a Southern family, been promoted to the rank of captain, and had acquired much property in North Carolina. When the war broke out, he was offered a much higher Confederate commission, but declined in order that he could stay in the U.S. Army. He received a commission of brigadier general of volunteers March 19, 1862.

Woodbury's commission was that of volunteers rather than an engineer commission. Brigadier General John Barnard discussed this point in his report of January 1863:

It will be thus seen that the Corps of Engineers as now organized does not furnish adequate rank even to command the limited number of engineer troops brought into the field. The engineers attached to the army corps (with the single exception of Lieutenant-Colonel Alexander, who derived his rank not from the corps, but from a law having no particular relation to engineers, and since repealed) were but lieutenants. In a European service the chief engineer serving with an army corps would be a field officer, generally a colonel.

There is a twofold evil in this want of rank: First, the great hardships and injustice to the officers themselves, for they have, almost without exception, refused or have been refused high positions in the volunteer service (to which they have seen their contemporaries of the other branches elevated) on the ground that their services as engineers were absolutely necessary. Second, it is an evil to the service, since an adequate rank is almost as necessary to an officer for the efficient discharge of his duties as professional knowledge. The engineer's duty is a responsible one. He is called upon to decide important questions, to fix the positions of defensive works (and thereby of the troops who occupy them,) to indicate the manner and points of attack of fortified positions. To give him the proper weight with those with whom he is associated he should have, as they have, adequate rank.[20]

This problem was not solved during the war, however. When the 1864 campaign began, the Army of the Potomac's chief of artillery was Brigadier General Henry Hunt; its chief quartermaster was Brigadier General Rufus Ingalls, but its chief engineer, James C. Duane, wore only the gold oak leaves of a major. He would, in fact, be ranked by the commander of the volunteer engineer brigade, even though he was chief engineer of the entire army.

Woodbury's brigade spent most of their time once they had landed in Virginia in construction projects, largely clearing roads, corduroying them so they could be used by heavy wagons, and building bridges over the endless number of streams and swamps found in the Peninsula. According to Barnard, the army's chief engineer,

The engineer equipage consisted of about 160 bateaux, or wooden pontoons of the French model, with the necessary balks, chess, anchors, cordage, &c. There were also a certain number (of which I do not now find any exact statement) of Birago trestles and Russian canvas boats. As originally got up, this bridge equipage was organized in trains, of which there were six regular trains, consisting each of thirty-four French pontoons and eight Birago trestles, calculated to make a bridge of about 250 yards in length, and an advanced guard train composed of Birago trestles and Russian canvas boats. The wagons for but four of the regular trains and for the advanced guard train were provided.[21]

As it turned out, these trains were broken up to fit specific bridging needs. As well, engineers used their pontoon boats as landing craft, a group of 250 officers and men of the 15th having been sent ashore onto the Peninsula before the infantry to pick a landing site and prepare to haul artillery ashore.

Furthermore, "Thirty wagons for engineer troops were prepared, containing the special tools required for engineer troops. Twenty of these accompanied the Engineer Brigade and ten accompanied the [regular U.S. Army's] Engineer Battalion." Barnard reported about equipment sent on the campaign.

Although McClellan's army was plenty large enough to easily take Richmond by following his well-thought-out plan, McClellan himself lacked the pluck to do the job. He let his fears of being outnumbered and destroying the beautiful army he had spent so long creating overwhelm him. His advance was very, very slow. Disease in the swampy land racked his army as well as Confederate bullets; the 15th New York lost two lieutenants to disease alone before the army reached the outskirts of Richmond.

"The campaign on the Peninsula called for great labor on the part of the engineers," Barnard reported.

> The country, notwithstanding its early settlement, was a *terra incognito*. We knew the York River and the James River, and we had heard of the Chickahominy, but this was about the extent of our knowledge. Our maps were so incorrect, that they were found to be worthless before we reached Yorktown. New ones had to be prepared, based on reconnaissances made by the officers of engineers. The siege of Yorktown involved great responsibility, besides exposure and toil. The movements of the whole army were determined by the engineers. The Chickahominy again arrested us, where, if possible, the responsibility and labor of the engineer officers were increased. In fact, everywhere and on every occasion, even to our last position at Harrison's Landing, this responsibility and labor on the part of the engineers was incessant.[22]

However, despite the constant slow advance, when Union advanced pickets could finally see the spire of St. Paul's Episcopal Church, the Confederates, whose wounded commander had been replaced by a scrapper named Robert E. Lee—another pre-war U.S. Army engineer—attacked. McClellan scrambled back towards a base where he could regroup. Although he handled the retreat masterfully, while Lee's troops struck with a remarkable lack of coordination and intelligence, the Union army still retreated.

The campaign had been very helpful for the engineers to determine what of their equipment worked, what didn't, and what would have to be changed. Barnard had not liked the Birago system of sectional pontoons; it, he had to report, "proved itself dangerous and unreliable—useful for an advance guard or detachment, unfit in general for a military bridge." The

French system McClellan initially favored proved far and away the most sturdy, reliable, and useful general military bridging system.[23]

As McClellan watched over his army licking its wounds on the James, Lincoln appointed another commander, John Pope, to gather troops around Washington and press south, at the same time ordering McClellan to abandon the Peninsula and join Pope's troops. McClellan moved at his usual snail's pace, thus missing another major Union defeat on the old Bull Run battleground. After leaving the Peninsula, McClellan sent the Engineer Brigade to garrison Fort Lyon, outside Alexandria, Virginia, as infantry.

Lee then drove north on a raid designed to take the war to his northern opponent, at the same time encouraging recruiting and supplies from supposed friendly Marylanders. McClellan was quickly restored to the command of the troops who had grown to love him the winter before. Handed a huge piece of luck when Lee's orders to his dispersed troops was found by some Union infantrymen, McClellan moved remarkably quickly for him, catching Lee dug in around the town of Sharpsburg and the Antietam Creek. There, in the bloodiest single day of the war, McClellan's uncoordinated attacks were held off by a hard-fighting Southern command. The two forces sat, watching each other warily, for a day, then Lee withdrew back into Virginia.

McClellan returned to his old sitting around and holding reviews habits, and, after pleading for some movement, Lincoln replaced him with one of his corps commanders, a Rhode Island inventor and businessman, Ambrose Burnside. Burnside planned a quick move overland directly at Richmond, depending on his forces moving before Lee could react. Initially, the move went well, but the order for the pontoon train to meet the army at the Rappahannock, so the engineers could bridge it before the infantry arrived, failed to get issued on time. The army waited for its pontoons.

Finally, on the afternoon of November 27, 1862, the pontoons arrived. Brainerd later wrote the brigade "could have thrown two bridges across the stream without opposition that night had been they been allowed to do so. There was no force of the enemy in the city, and General Longstreet, with the advance of the Confederate army, had by a forced march occupied a portion of the heights in rear of the city on the 21st."[24]

Burnside, however, became a bit lethargic, and it was some weeks until he finally gave the order to build the bridges. Most of his officers and men, by that point, thought that an attack across the river, through the town of Fredericksburg, and up over the heights, protected in many spots by stone walls, would be suicidal. But Burnside could not be dissuaded.

The engineers built their bridges under fire from Mississippi infantrymen in Fredericksburg who were finally driven off by Union infantrymen who used pontoons as assault boats to cross the river and take the town. The bridges up, the infantry crossed, many to their deaths. The assault was a failure. Burnside then tried a flank move, but it got totally bogged down in Virginia's December mud, despite the best effort of engineer road builders.

In March of 1863, General Woodbury, apparently worn down by his labors as commander of the Engineer Brigade, was sent on to command the District of Key West and Tortugas in the Department of the Gulf. There, further attacked by yellow fever, he died on August 15, 1864.

Woodbury's replacement was a professional soldier and military engineer, Henry Washington Benham. Benham, who had been born in Connecticut on April 17, 1813, had been a member of the West Point class of 1837 from where he had gone directly into the Corps of Engineers. He served in the Mexican War and had been offered a chance at a promotion in 1855 that would have required his transfer to the infantry—a chance he rejected in order to stay in the Corps.

When the war broke out, Benham served as chief engineer in the Department of the Ohio, taking part in the West Virginia campaign that gained McClellan his first fame. Benham followed McClellan up the ladder, earning a star as a brigadier general of volunteers. His first instinct to stay in the engineers proved a wise one, as his star was tarnished in the failed campaign around Charleston, South Carolina, in 1862, when he ordered an attack upon Confederate works as Secessionville against the advice of his subordinates. The assault failed, with deadly results. He was removed from command and returned to Washington with a revoked commission. Lincoln, however, canceled the revocation, and Benham was given another chance as brigade commander, this time in charge of the Volunteer Engineer Brigade.

As well, on March 3, 1863, Congress recognized that officers of both the Corps of Engineers and Corps of Topographical Engineers effectively did the same work in the field and abolished the latter organization, sending its members into a larger Corps of Engineers. With this merger, the duties of the Corps were greatly enlarged. According to an officer later,

> The duties required of the corps during the war were multitudinous, but consisted principally in planning, tracing, and superintending the construction of all fortifications, of whatever nature, needed in military operations, whether these works were of a temporary or permanent character; and also in planning, laying-out, and constructing all works needed for the attack or the defense of fortifications. The corps was charged with the duty of securing and reporting upon the topographical features of the country through which the armies were operating, to the extent of furnishing maps and detailed descriptions sufficiently clear and accurate to permit the commanding generals to order the movement of troops with certainty as to the ground over which these troops were to maneuver.[25]

After the unsuccessful "Mud March" into Virginia, Burnside was replaced by another corps commander, Joseph Hooker. Hooker, whose nickname "Fighting Joe" came from an inadvertent newspaper headline, planned to swing around Lee's left and catch him coming out of the defenses of Fredericksburg. Again, engineers were vital in setting up pontoon bridges to cross the Rappahannock, although many of the cavalry and infantry troops would actually cross upriver by fords. During this campaign, Benham reported, the brigade, between April 28 and May 4, laid 14 pontoon bridges, covering all the fords upriver from Fredericksburg as well as at Fredericksburg itself. Most of these were "ordinary wood pontoons," although one laid across the river at Franklin's Crossing, some three miles below Fredericksburg, was a canvas pontoon.[26]

In the most brilliantly fought, and most unusual, battle of his career, Lee left some troops to defend Fredericksburg, while his main body met Hooker's men near Chancellorsville. Then, Hooker stalled, Lee sent Jackson with his corps to sneak around Hooker's right and destroy the Army of the Potomac. The attack went on magnificently, with the Union XI Corps running away in almost total disarray.

Then, the Union army driven from Virginia's soil, Lee led another Northern raid, with the purposes of keeping Federals from Virginia for the rest of the year, as well as taking the burden of supplying the Army of Northern Virginia from the fields of Northern farmers instead of Southern ones. His forces and those of the Army of the Potomac's new commander, Major General George Gordon Meade, came together at the crossroads town of Gettysburg, Pennsylvania.

There Lee's troops were stopped cold over three days of hard fighting. Lee had to withdraw. Meade followed cautiously, allowing Lee to escape, much to Lincoln's ire. In late 1863 Meade advanced towards Lee, and the two armies sparred cautiously, rather like two battered boxers who were as much afraid of the other boxer than losing the fight. After Meade's abortive Mine Run Campaign, the Army of the Potomac withdrew to the Washington area to regroup, retrain, and prepare for the 1864 Campaign. On October 9, 1863, the few men who had signed up for the never-completed 2nd New York Volunteer Engineer Regiment, found themselves transferred into the 15th New York.

The campaign of 1864 would be conducted under the eye of a general brought east from a series of victories in the West, Major General U.S. Grant. Grant had been named commander of all the Union forces. He sent Sherman towards Atlanta in the West, while having other troops move through the Shenandoah Valley and up to Richmond from a James River landing. But Grant himself chose to place his headquarters with the Army of the Potomac, which was directly under Meade's command, to finish the war.

The year 1864 was a presidential election year. The army's old, defeated commander McClellan was the presidential candidate against Lincoln. McClellan ran as a Democrat, representing a party whose platform denounced continuing the war, although McClellan distanced himself from that plank. It was, however, important if the Union were to survive, that 1864 be a successful year for Federal arms. Training would have to be serious and hard over the winter.

The Engineer Brigade was sent to Washington for its preparations. The next year promised to be a hard one.

CHAPTER 2
Preparing for the End

October 1863 found the Volunteer Engineer Brigade in Washington under command of General Benham. The brigade consisted of two units, the 15th and 50th New York Volunteer Engineer Regiments, although the 15th was at only battalion strength. Brigade strength was at 36 officers and 834 enlisted men present for duty on October 20, 1863. By 20 November this number had fallen to 32 officers and 719 enlisted men.[1]

The Engineer Brigade was assigned to a camp by itself where it would have room enough for barracks, along with a drill field for infantry drill and water for training in building pontoon bridges. The Engineer Depot, as their camp was called, was located a half mile north of the Navy Yard on the right bank of the Potomac, around the foot of 14th and 15th Streets in Washington, which would be approximately where the entrance to the Maryland side of Long Bridge was.

"The winter-quarters of the engineers were, perhaps, the most unique of any in the army," an artilleryman enviously recalled. "In erecting them they gave their mechanical skill full play. Some of their officers' quarters were marvels of rustic design. The houses of one regiment in the winter of '63–4 were fashioned out of the straight cedar, which, being undressed, gave the appearance of a quaint but attractive and comfortable appearance."[2]

As part of its preparations for the upcoming campaign, many men received new weapons. The 50th turned in its light-weight Austrian rifled muskets and received short British-made copies of the British army's short rifle. These unique rifles, which came with a brass-hilted saber bayonet rather than the iron triangular spike bayonet used on rifled muskets, were carried by sergeants in the British service, as well as certain select rifle regiments. Some men of the 15th, which had earlier been issued high-quality British-made copies of the P1853 Enfield rifled musket, received new French-made 0.58 caliber rifled muskets.

Special Order No. 86, Washington Oct 13th. 1863

Private Orley R. Gorton, Co F 50th N.Y.V.E. is hereby detailed for duty in the Qr. Mr Dept. Engineer Brigade, and will report to Capt Caslow A.Q.M. as soon as possible.

The quartermaster of the brigade was responsible not only for issuing all equipment to the men of the brigade, but reconnoitering an area before the brigade marched to it and laying out a camp area before the men and equipment arrived there. Generally a captain served as assistant quartermaster.

Special Order No. 87 Washington Oct 16th 1863

I. - Privates John McKeon & James Lee Co "B." 15th N.Y.V.E. on duty in the Ambulance Corps Engineer Brigade, are hereby returned to their regiment.

I.I - The Commanding Officer 15th N.Y.V.E. will detail two good men to report to Lieut John L. Roosa for duty in the Ambulance Corps until further orders.

Originally during battle musicians from regimental bands were supposed to bring wounded men back to aid stations and field hospitals. Untrained and not under direct medical officers' supervision, musicians proved poor medics. Therefore, on August 2, 1862, the Army of the Potomac ordered an official Ambulance Corps with permanently assigned men under medical corps command. Each regiment had three ambulances pulled by two horses each, all commanded by a sergeant. A second lieutenant, in this case John L. Roosa, commanded the ambulances, each staffed with a driver and two stretcher-bearers, in the brigade.

Special Order No. 88. Washington D.C. Oct 28th. 1863

I. - Private Alex Anderson 15th N.Y.V.E. on duty in the Q.M. Dept Engr. Brigade, is hereby returned to this regiment.

I.I. - Private Frederick Butterfield Co. "C" 50th N.Y.V. Engrs. is hereby detailed for duty in the Qr Mr Dept of this Brigade and will report to Capt. I.F. Caslow A.Q.M. as soon as possible.

General Order No. 53: Washington DC, Oct 31, 1863

The Comd'g General will review and inspect this Brigade at 10 a.m. tomorrow on the ground near the Lincoln Hospital. The officers will be mounted, and the men will have all their equipments, blankets rolled and knapsacks packed.

A full inspection was to be done on the last day of every month, according to Army Regulations. The inspection was done in open order, with the men completely equipped as for a campaign. On the arrival of an inspecting officer in front of the company, the men were brought to attention and the inspector walked along the ranks, "minutely" inspecting "the arms, accouterments, and dress of each soldier." When this was finished, the company commander ordered his men to open their cartridge boxes, and the inspector examined the ammunition. Finally, the captain ordered his men to unsling and open their knapsacks. "The knapsacks will be placed at the feet of the men, the flaps from them, with the great-coats on the flaps, and the knapsacks leaning on the great-coats. In this position, the Inspector will examine their contents, or so many of them as he may think necessary,...with the non-commissioned officers, the men standing at attention."[3]

Special Order No. 89, Washington D.C. October 31st. 1863

Private W. Reeves Co. K 50th. N.Y.V. Engineers on duty in the Commissary Dept Engineer Brigade is hereby returned to his regiment.

The Commissary Department, also known as the Subsistence Department, was that group that provided food to the men in any given unit.

Special Order No. 90, Washington D.C. Nov 2nd. 1863

I. Private Lewis Soper Co. "B." 50th. N.Y.V.E. on duty at these Head Quarters is hereby returned to his regiment.

I.I - Private Harrison Dodge Co. D. 50th N.Y.V.E. is hereby detailed for duty in the Qr. Mr. Dept of this Brigade, and will report to Capt. J.F. Caslow A.Q.M. as soon as possible.

General Order No. 54, Washington DC, Nov. 4, 1863

In future the Officers of the Guard will immediately after the old guard is relieved select one reliable man from each relief who shall load and cap his musket and who shall be posted over the prisoners also the supernumeraries who take charge of the prisoners when they leave the Guard House shall have their muskets loaded and capped.

To further ensure the safe keeping of the prisoners the officer of the guard shall verify the number of prisoners in the Guard House at every relief.

Special Order No. 91, Washington Nov 5th. 1863

A Board of survey consisting of

        Capt. T. Lubey   15th N.Y.V. Engrs &
        Lieut I. Haven   Do

is hereby convened to audit the accounts, make inventories and report on the condition of public property in the possession of Walter C. Cassin deceased, late Major of the 15th N.Y.V. Engrs.

According to the 94th Article of War, "When any commissioned officer shall die or be killed in the service of the United States, the major of the regiment, or the officer doing the major's duty in his absence, or in any post or garrison, the second officer in command, or the assistant military agent, shall immediately secure all his effects or equipage, then in camp or quarters, and shall make an inventory thereof, and forthwith transmit the same to the office of the Department of War, to the end that his executors or administrators may receive the same."[4]

Special Order No. 92 November 9th, 1863

In compliance with Gen. Orders No 91. from the War Department July 29th 1862 XI Sec &. Major Wesley Brainerd of the 50th N.Y.V.E. is hereby impowered to try and sentence prisoners of the 15th N.Y.V.E. who are to be tried by Regimental Court Martial there being no Field Officer at present serving with the 15th.

According to Army Regulations governing courts-martial, Major Brainerd would, being the senior member of this particular court of the 15th, become the president of the court. He would be joined by between 4 and 12 other members who would be lower in rank.

Special Order No 93 Washington Nov 13th. 1863

A Board of Survey to consist of -
> Lieutenant G.W. Nares, A.C.S.
> Lieutenant H.P. Curtis, A.D.C.
> Lieutenant P.C. Kingsland A.D.C..

is hereby ordered to convene at the Hd. Qrs. Engineer Brigade A.-o-P. on the 14th instant for the purpose of inspecting and valuing a horse said to belong to Capt W.C. Chester,- said horse offered for sale to the Quarter Masters Department

General Order No. 55, Washington, Nov. 16, 1863

That no misunderstanding on the subject may exist the General Commanding wishes it to be distinctly understood that the camps of the two regiments of this command will form a single encampment for the police and discipline of which the senior regimental officer is Col. W.H. Pettes [who] will be responsible as Commandant of Camp - to the General Commanding the brigade and such rules as he may prescribe for said police and discipline or permits to be absent from camp for men and for officers - the latter not to be absent without the approval of the commander of their [regiment], as also of said commandant of camp - will be obeyed and respected accordingly.

It being understood that for any absence of an officer from the usual prescribed duties of drill or inspection - or during a night - the further authority from these Head Quarters is necessary.

Colonel Pettes commanded the 50th. He would remain in Washington during the upcoming campaign, however, commanding the Engineer Depot in which equipment was made. Lieutenant Colonel Ira Spaulding would be the field commander of the 50th.

Special Order No. 94 Washington D.C. Nov 16th 1863

Major W.A. Ketchum having reported for duty is hereby assigned to the command of the Battalion of the 15th N.Y.V.E.

Capt. Jos. Wood jr will on the receipt of this order turn over the command, papers etc. to Major Ketchum.

General Order No. 56, Washington, DC, Nov. 17, 1863

General Orders No. 45 of Sept 28th from these Head Qtrs. are hereby changed as follows.

Reveille	6 a.m.	Dinner	12 m
Police	6 1/2/ a.m.	Drill Infy	3 to 4 p.m
Breakfast	7 "	Dress Parade	4 1/2 "
Sick Call	7 1/2 a.m.	Supper	5 1/2 p.m
Guard Mounting	9 "	Tattoo	8 "
Drill Infantry	9 1/2 to 11 1/2 a.m.	Taps	8 1/2 "

Special Order No. 95, Washington D.C. Nov 17th. 1863

I. - Special Orders No 92 Nov 9th 1863 from these Head Quarters, are hereby annulled.

I.I - In conformity with Gen Orders No 91, from the War Department July 29th. 1862 X. Sec 7. Major W.A. Ketchum of the 15th N.Y.V. Engrs is hereby empowered to try and sentence prisoners of the 15th N.Y.V.E. who are ordered to be tried by Regimental Court Martial

The senior officer in a regiment or battalion was always to serve as president in a court-martial of that unit's own men unless he were a witness or had pressed the charges.

Special Order No. 96 Washington D.C. Nov 19th 1863

Private Luther Staley Co G, 50th N.Y.V. Engrs. is hereby detailed for duty as harness maker in the Q M. Dept and will report to Capt Caslow A.Q.M. as soon as possible.

Special Order No. 97 Washington D.C. Nov 23rd 1863

Corporal Peter Cady Co. "A" 15th N.Y.V.E. is hereby detailed for duty as guard at these Head Quarters until further orders and will report as soon as possible.

General Order No. 57, Washington DC, Nov. 24th/63

In compliance with the request of the Governor of the State of New York Thursday next the 26th instant will be observed by the Regiments of this command as a day of Thanksgiving.

On that day there will be no drills or work of any kind performed that can be avoided.

Although a day devoted to thanksgiving and prayer had been noted as early as the first winter in Plymouth colony, it was not until 1830 that New York adapted the holiday as an annual custom. Although other states followed New York's lead, still it was not until 1864 that Thanksgiving became a national holiday, when President Abraham Lincoln named the fourth Thursday in November a day of national thanksgiving. In this instance the New York custom was being followed in this brigade of New Yorkers.

Special Order No 98. Washington D.C. Nov 24th. 1863.

I. - Private Bartholemew Burke Co. "C" 50th N.Y. E. on duty in the Ambulance Corps Engineer Brigade, is hereby returned to his company.

I.I. - Private James Boyd Co. "C" 50th N.Y.V.E. is hereby detailed for duty in the Ambulance Corps and will report immediately to Lieut I.L. Roosa.

Special Order No. 99 Washington D.C. Nov 29th/63

A Military Commission, consisting of
Col W.H. Pettes 50th N.Y.V. Engineers
Major Wesley Brainerd "   "
Major W.A. Ketchum 15th "   "
is hereby ordered to assemble at once at such place as the senior officer may designated, to examine the papers of Lt John T. Davidson 50th N.Y.V.E. who has been reported absent from his Regiment "without leave," and to determine whether he was absent from proper and sufficient cause.

General Order No. 58, Washington DC, Dec 6th, 1863

Owing to the prevalence of Small Pox in the neighborhood of this camp it is directed that all persons connected with this Brigade be immediately vaccinated - and it is especially enjoined upon the Officers to see that all the men in their respective commands attend to this at once.

According to regulations, recruits were to be vaccinated, but this rarely happened. Moreover, the need for regular re-vaccination for smallpox was not appreciated by doctors of the period, although some men did make arrangements to have this done. Statistically, the army reported some five cases of smallpox per thousand men during the war.

General Order No. 59, Washington DC, Dec 7th 1863

Until further orders there will be a ponton drill by the Brigade on Monday Wednesday and Friday Afternoons when the weather permits. The Senior - Field Officer - present for duty will take command of the drills.

General Order No. 60, Washington DC, Dec 7th, 1863

The Comd'g General has noticed a great want of attention to the Infantry drills, and in future it is especially directed that the Comd'g Officer of the Regiment shall see that each Company of his command which goes out to drill is accompanied by or - is under - the command of a Commissioned Officer. If there [are] not men enough to make a comy. [company-grade, i.e., a captain or lower] Officer - command, the squad must be attached to another company and not sent out under a non-comy. Officer, - and in the case of the deficiency of comr. officers so that one such officer cannot be assigned to each Co. - two or more companies will be united as far as may be necessary for this purpose.

Although specialists, engineer troops were to be trained to serve as infantry and, indeed, this training would be needed by many of the New York engineers in the upcoming campaign. Recalled an artilleryman of the two New York engineer regiments, "These engineers went armed as infantry for purposes of self-defence only, for fighting was not their legitimate business, nor was it expected of them. There were emergencies in the history of the army when they were drawn up in line of battle."[5]

Special Order No. 100 Washington D.C. Dec 9th. 1863.

Private Christopher Welse Co. "A" 15th N.Y.V. Engineers is hereby detailed for duty as saddler in the Q.M. Dept of this Brigade and will report immediately to Capt I.J. Caslow A.Q.M.

Special Order No. 101 Washington D.C. Dec 10th/63

I. - Paragraph 2 of S.O. No 98 of Nov 24th 1863 from these Hd. Qrs. is hereby revoked.

I.I. - Private James Hegland Co. G. 50th N.Y.V.E. is hereby detailed for duty in the Ambulance Corps of this Brigade, and will report to Lt. I.L. Roosa until further orders.

Special Order No. 102 Washington D.C. Dec 12th 1863

Private Alonzo Lyons Co. K 50th. N.Y.V.E. on duty in the Q.M. Dept of this Brigade is hereby returned to his regiment.

Special Order No. 103 Washington D.C. Dec 15th 1863

Col W.H. Pettes 50th N.Y.V.E. is hereby directed to proceed to the camp of the Detachment of his Regiment near Rappahannock Station and also to the Head Qrs of the Army of the Potomac for the purpose of transacting business.

Co. Pettes will return to this camp as soon as he has accomplished the purpose of his visit.

On December 19 Lieutenant Thomas J. Owen, 50th New York, then stationed with the regiment's detachment on the Rappahannock Station, wrote home: "At present, I am on duty on the road between here and Bealton which a large number of infantry are repairing by building corduroy bridges, etc. Captain Folwell has charge of the whole detail, and I go out to superintend certain jobs which they will not do well if they are not watched. I like General Meade's plan of fixing the roads. It gives him a great advantage on the move, especially if it is in a wet time."[6]

General Order No. 61, Washington Dec. 20th, 1863

The usual monthly inspection will take place Monday Dec 21st at 10 a.m.

Commandants of Companies will have reports prepared in the form prescribed by the A.I. Gen. for the inspection of November.

Special Order No. 104 Washington D.C. Dec 26th 1863

I. - Private Luther Staley, 50th. Regt. N.Y.V. Engineers on duty in the Brigade Qr. Mr. Department, is returned to his regiment.

I.I. - Capt S. Chester A.I. Genl. [Acting Inspector General] is hereby ordered to proceed with clerk and Orderly to the camp of the Detachment of this Brigade near Rappahannock Station on business.

Having completed his business Capt Chester will return immediately to this camp.

The inspector general's office was responsible for reporting the discipline of the troops; their instruction in all military exercises and duties: the state of their arms, clothing, equipments, and accoutrements of all kinds; of their kitchens and messes; of the barracks and quarters at the post; of the guard-house, prisons, hospital, bake-house, magazines, store-houses, and stores of every description; of the stables and horses; the condition of the post school; the management and application of the post and company funds; the state of the post, and regimental, and company books, papers, and files; the zeal and ability of the officers in command of the troops; the capacity of the officers conducting the administrative and staff services, the fidelity and economy of their disbursements; the condition of all public property, and the amount of money in the hands of each disbursing officer; the regularity of issues and payments; the mode of enforcing discipline of courts-martial, and by the authority of the officers; the propriety and legality of all punishments inflicted; and any information whatsoever concerning the service, in any matter or particular that may merit notice, or aid to correct defects or introduce improvements.[7]

Special Order No. 105 Washington D.C. Dec. 26th 1863

In compliance with orders from the General in-Chief dated Dec 23rd. 1863, Lieut P.C. Kingland A.D.C. [aide-de-camp] will immediately proceed to join his Regt. wherever it may be.

Special Order No. 106 Washington Dec 29th 1863

Leave of absence is granted to the following named Officers:

Capt Geo. W. Ford - - - 50th N.Y.V. Engineers for ten (10) days commencing January 1st. 1864.

"Applications for leaves of absence...to officers of engineers...for more than thirty days, must be referred to the Adjutant-General for the decision of the Secretary of War."[8]

General Order No. 62, Washington D.C. Dec 30th 1863

Commanding Officers of Regiments and Detachments of this Brigade, will muster their men for pay on the 31st inst.

Special Order No. 107 Washington Dec 30th 1863

Leave of absence is granted to the following named Officer:
Captain Channing Clapp Asst. Adjt. General for fifteen (15) days.

Special Order No 108 Washington Dec 30th 1863.

Private John I. Slattery Co. C. 15th N.Y.V.E. is hereby detailed for duty as clerk in the Asst. Inspector General's Office of this Brigade until further orders. Detail to date from Dec 23rd 1863

General Order No. 63, Washington DC Dec. 31st 1863

I. - 1st Lieut Frank S. Livingston 15th N.Y. V. Engrs. is hereby appointed aid-de-camp to the General Commanding the Brigade to rank as such from the first day of January 1864, and he will be obeyed and respected accordingly.

I - I. - Lieut Livingston A.D.C. is hereby appointed Acting Assistant Adjutant General of the Engineer Brigade during the absence of the Assistant Adjutant General of the Brigade.

Aides-de-camp were "confidential officers selected by general officers to assist them in their military duties.... Attached to the person of the general, they receive orders only from him. Their functions are difficult and delicate. Often enjoying the full confidence of the general, they are employed in representing him, in writing orders, in carrying them in person if necessary, in communicating them verbally upon battle-fields and other fields of manoeuvre."[9] Each brigadier general was authorized one aide-de-camp.

The duties of the assistant adjutant general of a brigade included: "publishing orders in writing; making up written instructions, and transmitting them; reception of reports and returns; disposing of them; forming tables, showing the state and position of corps; regulating details of service; corresponding with the administrative departments relative to the wants of troops; corresponding with the corps, detachments, or individual officers serving under the orders of the same commander; and the methodical arrangement and care of the records and papers of his office."[10]

General Order No. 64, Washington D.C. Dec 31 1863

January 1st 1864 will be observed as a Holiday by this command and no drills or usual duties will be required of Officers and men - other than those required by Regulations for the Army at all times.

General Order No. 65, Washington D.C. Dec 31st 1863

I - Before a Regimental Court Martial, of which Major W.A. Ketchum is President convened at Hd. Qrs. 15th Regt. N.Y.V.E. in pursuance of Special Orders No 95. C.S. from Hd. Qrs. Engr Brigade, were arraigned and tried.

1st Private Peter Mulligan, Co. B, 15th N.Y.V.E. on the following charges.

Charge. "Running the Guard."
Finding "Guilty"
Sentence - That he forfeit one months pay and be compelled to perform his guard or other duty with a knapsack weighing at least fifty pounds and that he be compelled to stand upon a barrel on the parade at the time of dress parade with the same knapsack for the space of thirty days, and that he be drilled with said knapsack, three hours each day, half in the morning, and half in the afternoon, on the double quick for the same period, and that he be reduced to a 2nd. class private from the 1st day of December.

2nd - Private Cornelius McDonald Co B 15th N.Y. V. Engrs. upon the following charges.

Charge - Conduct prejudicial to good order and military discipline
Finding "Guilty"
Sentence. That he forfeit one months pay and be compelled to perform all his guard and other duties with a knapsack weighing not less than fifty pounds for the space of thirty days and that he be compelled to stand upon a barrel, with the said knapsack on the parade of his regiment at the time of dress parade and be compelled to drill three hours each day, half in the morning and the other half in the afternoon on the double quick, with said knapsack, for the same period of thirty days.

3rd - Private Jacob Knight of Co B 15th N.Y.V.E. on the following charge

Charge "Absence without leave"
Finding "Guilty"
Sentence To forfeit one months pay, and be compelled to perform his guard and other duty, with a knapsack weighing not less than fifty pounds for the period of thirty days, and that he be reduced to second class private from December 1st.

4th Private James Lee of Co B 15th N.Y.V.E. on the following charge.

Charge "Absence without leave"
Finding "Guilty"
Sentence That he forfeit one months pay and be compelled to perform all his guard or other duties with a knapsack, weighing not less than fifty pounds and that he be compelled to stand upon a barrel on the parade of his regiment at the time of dress parade with

said knapsack for the space of thirty days and that he be drilled with said knapsack three hours a day, half in the morning and the other half in the afternoon on the double quick for the same period.

5th Private James King Co "B" 15th N.Y.V.E. on the following charge

Charge	Absence without leave
Finding	"Guilty"

Sentence   That he forfeit one months pay and be reduced to 2nd. class from Dec 1st and that he be compelled to perform his guard or other duty with a knapsack weighing not less than fifty pounds for the period of thirty days.

6th - Private Charles Colligan Co B. 15th N.Y.V.E. on the following charge.

Charge	"Absence without leave"
Finding	"Not guilty

and the court does therefore acquit the accused Private Charles Colligan.

7th. - Daniel Brown - Co "B" 15th N.Y.V.E. on the following charge

Charge	"Drunkenness"
Finding	"Guilty"

Sentence: That he forfeit one months pay, and be compelled to perform his guard and other duty with a knapsack weighing not less than fifty pounds and that he be compelled to stand upon a barrel on the parade, at the time of dress parade, with the same knapsack and a placard on his breast with "For Drunkenness," in large letters for the space of thirty days, and that he be drilled with said knapsack for three hours in each day, half in the morning and half in the afternoon, in the double quick for the same period.

8th. - Private John S. White Co B. 15th N.Y.V.E. on the following charges.

Charge 1st.	"Drunkenness"
Charge 2nd	Conduct prejudicial to good order and military discipline
Finding 1st	"Guilty"
Finding 2nd	"Guilty"

Sentence   That he forfeit one months pay and be tied up by the thumbs on the public parade so that his toes will just touch the ground, his body, his body and arms extended to their utmost length between the hours of reveille and tattoo, for the period of twenty days with the word "Loafer" on a placard on his breast in plain large letters, and that he be reduced to a 2nd class man to date from Nov 1st 1863

9th - Private Charles O. Leverick Co. "C" 15th N.Y.V.E. on the following charge.

Charge   "Absence without leave"
Finding   "Guilty"
Sentence   That he forfeit one months pay and be reduced to a second class private to date from December 1st and be compelled to perform his guard and other duty with a knapsack weighing not less than fifty pounds for the space of thirty days and that he be drilled with said knapsack three hours each day, half in the morning and half in the afternoon at the double quick for the same period.

10th. Artificer W.H. Daly Co C. 15th N.Y.V.E. on the following charge,
Charge   "Absence without leave,"
Finding   "Guilty"
Sentence: That he forfeit one months pay and be compelled to perform his guard and other duty with a knapsack weighing not less than fifty pounds for the period of thirty days and that he be reduced to a 2nd class private from December 1st and be drilled with said knapsack three hours each day, half in the morning and half in the afternoon at the double quick for the said period of thirty days.

11th - Private James Porter Co "A, 15th N.Y.V.E. on the following charges
Charge 1st   "Absence without leave"
Charge 2nd   Conduct prejudicial to good order and military discipline
Finding   "Guilty"
Sentence: That he forfeit one months pay and be compelled to perform his guard or other duty with a knapsack weighing not less than fifty pounds and that he be compelled to stand upon a barrel on the regimental parade at the time of evening parade with the same knapsack for the space of thirty days and that he be drilled with said knapsack three hours each day half in the morning and half in the afternoon, at the double quick for the same period.

I.I. - The proceedings of the Regimental Court Martial in the foregoing cases having been transmitted to the General Commanding the Brigade the following are the orders thereon.

In the case of Private Peter Colligan Co B - Private Cornelius McDonald Co B - Artificer W.H. Daily Co C - Private James Porter Co "A" - the findings & sentences are approved so far as the forfeiture of pay and the other punishment for five days only.

In the case of Private Knight Co B. the findings and sentence is approved as to forfeiture of pay and drill as therein ordered for two days only.

In the case of Private James Lee Co B. the finding and sentence is approved as to forfeiture of pay and drill for four days.

In the case of James B. King the sentence is remitted except as to the forfeiture of pay for one month.

In the case of Private Charles Colligan the proceedings of the court are approved.

In the case of Daniel Brown, the proceedings and sentence of the court are approved except the last clause commencing with the words - "and that he be drilled".

In the case of Private John S. White - the sentence is approved except that in place of the words "his toes will just touch the ground" will be inserted "he shall stand firmly on the ground."

In the case of Charles E. Leverick - the sentence is remitted except that he will forfeit one half months pay only - there being no justive evidence of his absence except the prisoners own plea of guilty.

The findings and sentences as approved will be carried into effect, the out-door punishment only, on such days as the weather will permit.

The Commanding General is thus lenient in remitting so much of the above sentences in the hope that the punishment thus awarded will be sufficient to deter the men of the regiment from these offenses so frequently repeated of late, should be disappointed in this the men of the command may rest assured that such remissions may not be expected in the future.

Memorandum to modify Gen Orders No. 65 of Dec 31st from these Hd. Qrs

The sentence of Private John S. White Co B - 15th N.Y.V.E. is hereby further remitted to read as follows.

That he forfeit one months pay and be tied up by the wrists on the public parade, so that his feet shall rest upon the ground, and his arms extended, for one hour every day on five separate days wearing at the time a placard on his breast - on which shall be written in plain large letters "Loafer." and that he be reduced to a 2nd class man to date from November 1st 1863.

Absence without leave and drunkenness were by far the most common offenses in the Union army.

CHAPTER 3
In Camp: January–April 1864

▶━━━━━━━◀

Special Orders No. 1, Washington, D.C. Jan 1st 1864

I. 2nd. Lieut Andrew Manger is hereby relieved from duty as Quartermaster of Ponton train in the field and will report without delay to his Regiment Stationed at Washington.

I.I. Major Spaulding will appoint an officer of the 50th Regt N.Y.V.E. to receive from Lieut Manger the Quarter Master and Engineer property, for which he now is responsible.

Special Orders No. 2, Washington Jan 2nd 1864

Leave of Absence is granted to the following named officers

Capt A.C. Palmer - - - 50th N.Y.V. Engineers for fifteen (15) days.

Special Orders No. 3, Washington Jan 3rd. 1864

I. Leave of absence is granted to the following named officers:

Dr. A. Clarke Baum - 1st. Asst Surgeon 50th N.Y.V.E. for ten (10) days.

I.I. The services of Capt M.H. McGrath 50th N.Y.V. Engrs being needed at Head Qrs. for the construction of the Barracks; Capt McGrath is hereby relieved from the necessary of rejoining his company, as previously ordered.

The regiment would be authorized a surgeon, rated as a major, and an assistant surgeon, rated as a captain. They would wear the old English letters U.S. within the wreath on their cap fronts instead of the silver castle of the engineers.

Special Orders No. 4 Washington Jan 4th 1864

Capt J.F. Caslow A.Q.M. Engineer Brigade is hereby ordered to proceed with clerk and orderly to the camp of the Detachment of this Brigade near Rappahannock Station on business.

Having completed his business Capt Caslow will return immediately to this camp.

I.I. - Leave of absence is granted to the following Officer: Capt Timothy Lubey 15th N.Y.V.E. for ten (10) days.

On January 5 Benham was advised by David McCallum, the military director and superintendent of railroads in Washington, that all the available trains were involved in bringing forage to the front and the engineer requisition for trains for 6 pontoons, 26 pontoon wagons, and 8 army wagons and a car load of other freight would be held up until the army's forage needs were met.

Special Orders No. 5 Washington D.C. Jan 7th 1864

Sergeant Miller of Co "A." 50th Regt. N.Y.V. Engrs. is hereby ordered to take charge of Engineer property about to be sent to detachment in the field, and to report with said property as soon as possible to Major Spaulding at Rappahannock Station and return as soon as possible.

General Orders No 1, Washington Jan 8th 1864

The attention of the officers of this command is specially directed to Par 451 of the U.S. Rev. [vised] Reg.[ulations] and its strict observance will, for the future, be rigidly enforced. Hereafter no official notice will be taken of communications not transmitted through this proper channel.

Paragraph 451:

All official correspondence between the heads of the different departments of the staff of any command, and its commander, must pass through the Adjutant-General, Assistant Adjutant-General, or Adjutant of the command, as the case may be. Communications to or from a commander, and those under his command, must pass through the Adjutant-General, Assistant Adjutant-General, or Adjutant on duty with it; excepting only such communications between a disbursing officer and the chief of his particular branch of the staff, as relate exclusively to the ordinary routine of business in their own department. All communications, whether from an inferior to a superior, or *vice versá*, are, as a general rule, to be passed through intermediate commanders. The same rule governs in verbal applications: for example, a Lieutenant seeking an indulgence must apply through his Captain, the Captain through the Adjutant, and so on.[1]

Special Orders No. 6 Washington Jan 8th 1864

I. Private Newton Wheeler Co "I" 50th N.Y.V.E. on duty in the Q.M. Dept of this Brigade, is hereby returned to his Regiment.

I.I.- Private Mathias M. Peterson Co. "G" 50th N.Y.V.E. is hereby detailed for duty in the Q.M. Dept of this Brigade and will report immediately to Capt Caslow A.Q.M.

Special Orders No. 7, Washington Jan 8th 1864

I. Capt Personius 50th N.Y.V.E. will on receipt of this order relieve Major Brainerd, field officer of the day until Guard Mounting Jan 9th.

I.I - Upon the recommendation of their Company Commanders, privates M. Murphy, McClintock, Saunders, & O'Brian all of Co "D." 15th N.Y.V.E. are hereby released from confinement, and restored by duty.

Special Orders No. 8 Washington Jan 11th 1864

Leave of absence is granted to the following named officers
1st. Lieut K.S. O'Keefe 15th N.Y.V.E. for ten (10) days.
2nd. Lieut Chas. F. Carroll 50th N.Y.V.E. for ten (10) days.

Special Orders No. 9 Washington Jan 12th. 1864

Sergeant C.M. Byram 50th N.Y.V.E. is hereby ordered to proceed with Engineer Material to the camp of the detachment of this brigade at Rappahannock Station, and return as soon as practicable.

Special Orders No. 10 Washington Jan 13th. 1864

Upon the recommendation of their Regtl. Commanders, Corpl. Ford and Cummings and Private McConnell 15th N.Y.V.E. are hereby released from arrest and restored to duty.

Special Orders No. 11 Washington Jan 14th 1864

1 - Sergeant John Townsend 50th N.Y.V. Engrs. is hereby ordered to proceed with Engineer Material to Rapahannock Station, and to report to Lt-Col Spaulding, as soon as possible.
Sergt. Townsend will return as practicable.

2 - Leave of absence is granted to the following named Officers
Lieut J.L. Roosa 50th N.Y.,V.E. (to commence Jan 16/64)
" D.M. Hulse, " " " for ten days.

3 - Private John O'Hara Co. C, 50th N.Y.V.E. on duty in the Qr. Mr. Dept. Engr Brigade is hereby returned to his regiment.

4 - Private Newton Wheeler Co I, 50th N.Y.V.E. is hereby detailed for duty in Q.M. Dept of this Brigade, and will report to Capt Caslow A.Q.M. as soon as possible.

General Orders No 2, Washington Jan 15th 1864

In future all officers of this command preferring charges for officer to be tried by Courts Martial will obtain a copy of the charges in their possession.

Special Orders No. 12 Washington D.C. Jan 15 1864

In consequence of the recommendation of their Commanding Officer, the general Commanding directs that Sergt Geo E. Tilley Co B, Thos. Burton Co C & Corpl Geo C. Stoddard Co B, of the 15th Regt. N.Y.V.E. placed in arrest for having overstaid their Furloughs, be released and restored to duty.

Special Orders No. 13 Washington Jan 18th 1864

Leave of Absence is granted to the following named Officer.
1st Lieut R.O'S. Burke 15th N.Y.V.E. for ten (10) days.

Special Orders No. 14 Washington Jan 19th 1864

1 - Private Geo. B. Smith Co C. 50th N.Y.V.E. is hereby detailed for duty at these Head Quarters.
2 - Leave of absence is granted to the following named Officer.
Lt F.W. Pettes 50th N.Y.V.E. for ten (10) days.

Special Orders No. 15 Washington Jan 21st 1864

Leave of absence is granted to the following named officer.
Capt W.V. Personius, 50th N.Y.V.E. for ten (10) days.

General Orders No 3 Washington D.C. Jan 22nd 1864

There will be an inspection by Regiments of the different commands in this Brigade on Saturday the 23rd inst. at 10 A.M. by the A.A. In. General - the 50th will be inspected on their parade ground.

The "A.A. In. General" was the "acting assistant inspector general."

Special Orders No. 16 Washington Jan 23rd 1864

1 - Leave of absence is granted to the following named officers
Capt Jos Wood jr - 15th N.Y.V. Engineers, for ten (10) days.
2 - A General Court Martial is hereby appointed to meet at the Camp of the 15th Regt N.Y.V. Engrs. at 10 O'clock A.M. on Monday the 25th day of January 1864, or as soon thereafter as practicable for the trial of Private Patrick O'Driscoll Co. C. 50th N.Y.V.E. and such other business as may be brought before it.

Detail for the Court

1	Major Wesley Brainerd	50th N.Y.V.E. - - President
2	Capt T. Lubey	15th " " " "
3	" D.F. Schenck	50th " " " "
4	Lieut - Wm. Henderson	15th " " " "
5	" Sewall Sergeant	15th " " " "
6	" J. W. Ryding	15th " " " "

Lieut Frank S. Livingston A.D.C. - Judge Advocate

No other officers than those named can be assembled without manifest injury to the service.

3 - Private A.W. Hyndman Co. B. 50th N.Y.V.E. is hereby detailed as clerk for the General Court Martial to assemble Jan 25th 1864 and will report to Lieut. Livingston A.D.C. & Judge Advocate for duty.

Special Orders No 17 Washington Jan 26th. 1864

1 - Leave of absence is granted to the following named officer -
1st. Lieut. P.C. Kingsland A.D.C. for ten (10) days.

2 - That part of Special Orders No 16 Par. 2 from these Head Quarters detailing Lt I.W. Ryding 15th N.Y.V.E. as member of the Genl. Court Martial now in session at the camp of the 15th N.Y.V.E. is hereby revoked, and Lieut Ryding will hereafter act as supernumerary member of said court.

Special Orders No 18 Washington Jan 28th. 1864

Leave of Absence is granted to the following named Officer
2nd. Asst Surgeon Lewis V. Beers 50th N.Y.V.E. for ten (10) days.

On January 31 Major Ira Spaulding who commanded the brigade's detachment at the Rappahannock Station, reported to General Benham:

During the past month there has been little in our operations worthy of note. Our men have been principally employed in work upon winter quarters, fencing and flooring corrals, corduroy roads, and repairs and renewals in pontoon trains. On the afternoon of the 4th instant I received orders to take up the lower pontoon bridge at this point, move my trains to headquarters Army of the Potomac, have the bridge at Welford's Ford ready to take up after the trains passed, and report in person to headquarters. After seeing the tents struck of all the command except one company, the teams hitched up, and the work of dismantling the lower bridge commenced, I proceeded to headquarters. There I found that it was proposed to send a force of 10,000 men (6,000 infantry and 4,000 cavalry) to operate against a force of the enemy supposed to be in Shenandoah Valley, and that the bridge train was required for crossing Shenandoah River near Front Royal. Nothing was decided, however, in relation to the movement, and as it was only intended that the trains should be ready, I immediately sent back word for the men to finish taking up the lower bridge and return to camp with the trains, keeping everything ready for starting the trains at short notice. It was finally arranged before I left headquarters that if the movement was ordered I should only furnish the trains with the transportation and everything necessary for the effective operations of the quartermaster's department, and that Captain Mendell with his men should proceed to Front Royal in charge of the trains. Everything pertaining to this train was for some days kept ready for an immediate start, but the movement was not ordered. We have still some work to do upon our trains to put them in perfect order, and some additional work in camp and in the corrals. When this is done I hope to be able to resume our drills in infantry tactics and sapping and mining.[2]

Special Orders No 19 Washington D.C. Feb 1st 1864

1 - Capt W.V. Personius 50th N.Y.V. Engrs. and Lieut R.O.S. Burke 15th N.Y.V.E. are hereby detailed as members of the General Court Martial now in session at the Camp of the 15th N.Y.V.E.

2 - In consequence of an order from the War Dept detailing Capt T. Lubey and Lieut Wm. Hinderson of the 15th N.Y.V.E. on recruiting service, these Officers are hereby relieved as members of the above General Court Martial.

There was no regular system of keeping a flow of recruits to regiments in the field. Instead from time to time detachments of officers and men were sent to the home regions to open an office, print up recruiting flyers, and eventually return to the regiment with as many volunteers, "fresh fish" as the men called them, as possible. Each detachment was to consist of a lieutenant, a noncommissioned officer, two privates, a drummer, and a fifer. The recruiting officer was required to make sure his volunteers received a medical examination in his presence, and he was authorized to hire a civilian doctor to perform the exam.

Special Orders No 20 Washington D.C. Feb 1st 1864

In accordance with General Orders No 88, of 1862 from the War Dept. the recruiting from the 15th New York Vols Engrs, authorized in Special Orders No 25 of 1864, Head Qrs Army of the Potomac, is hereby increased by the addition of Sergt Bartholomew I. Daly of Co "A". Sergt Daily will proceed immediately to New York and report to Capt T. Lubey commanding recruiting detail.

Special Orders No 21 Washington D.C. Feb 3rd 1864

1 - Leave of Absence is granted to the following named officer Major W.A. Ketchum - 15th N.Y.V. Engineers for seven (7) days.

Special Orders No 22 Washington D.C. Feb 4th. 1864

1 - Leave of Absence is granted to the following named officers Lieut James L. Robbins - 50th Regt N.Y.V. Engrs. for ten (10) days.

Special Orders No 23 Washington D.C. Feb 5th 1864

Leave of Absence is granted to the following named Officers.
Capt M.H. McGrath 50th N.Y.V. Engineers for ten (10) days.

Special Orders No 24 Washington D.C. Feb 6th. 1864

During the absence of Major W.A. Ketchum 15th N.Y.V.E. Capt Joseph Wood jr 15th N.Y.V.E. will act as Field Officer for the trial of cases brought before a Regimental Court Martial.

Special Orders No 25 Washington D.C. Feb 9th 1864

I - Private Truman Ellis Co. C. 50th N.Y.V.E. on duty in the Qr Mrs Dept of this Brigade is hereby returned to his regiment.

I.I. - Private Wm. Brown Co. C. 15th N.Y.V.E. is hereby detailed for duty in the Qr Mr Dept of this Brigade, and will report immediately to Capt Caslon for duty.

Special Orders No 26 Washington D.C. Feb 10th 1864

1 - Private Peter Baumis Co "F" 50th N.Y.V.E. on duty in the Commissary Dept. is hereby returned to his Regt.

2 - Private Charles D. Wright Co. C. 50th N.Y.V.E. is hereby detailed for duty in the Q.M. Dept of this Brigade and will report immediately to Capt Caslow A.Q.M.

3 - Private Robert Roberts Co. C. 15th N.Y.V.E. is hereby detailed for duty in the Commissary Dept. of this Brigade, and will report immediately to Lt Wares A.C.S.

4 - Private B. Rogers Co. D. 15th N.Y.V.E. is hereby detailed as a clerk for the Genl. Court Martial now in session at Camp of 15th N.Y.V.E. and will report immediately to Lt Livingston Judge Advocate for duty.

5 - During the temporary absence of Lieut F.S. Livingston Judge Advocate, Lieut Sewall Sergeant 15th N.Y.V.E. member of the Genl. Court Martial, now sitting at the Camp of the 15th N.Y.V.E. will act as Judge Advocate of said Court.

The judge advocate at a court-martial was, although not necessarily a lawyer, the court legal officer. He summoned the witnesses to the trial and questioned them, essentially on behalf of the people, as well as advising the court's president on legal matters and making sure the defendant's rights were respected. Finally, he had to sign the records of the trial and transmit the official proceedings to the higher officer who had the authority to confirm the sentence, in this case General Benham.

Special Orders No 27 Washington D.C. Feb 14th 1864

Leave of Absence is granted to the following named Officers
Lieut A.H. Megay 15th N.Y.V. Engineers for ten (10) days.

Special Orders No 28 Washington D.C. Feb 13th 1864

1 - Private Joseph Snyder Co. C. and Christopher Welch Co A. 15th N.Y.V.E. on duty in the Q.M. Dept of this Brigade, are hereby returned to their regiment.

2 - Private Michael Gregory Co. C. 15th N.Y.V.E. is hereby detailed as saddler in the Qr Mr. Dept. and will report immediately to Capt Caslow A.Q.M. for duty.

3 - Private H. Craig Co "L." 50th. N.Y.V.E. is hereby detailed for duty as saddler in the Q.M. Dept. and will report immediately to Capt Caslow A.Q.M. for duty.

4 - Major W.A. Ketchum Comd'g 15th N.Y.V.E. is hereby appointed a member of the Council of Administration appointed by Special Orders No 68, Aug 17th. 1863 Par 3, from these Head Quarters.

The Council will assemble on the 15th inst or as soon thereafter as practicable to transact such business as may be brought before them.

On February 14 Sergeant Owen wrote home from his post on the Rappahannock Station: "Today is Sunday. We have had our inspection of arms, likewise of tents. Found everything in good condition. The company is well and contains, in all, 101 men, 80 of which are present. The twenty two [*sic*] are on detach[ed] service, absent with leave, sick, etc., Things are very quiet in camp. Today there is no work going on and the men show respect for the Sabbath by refraining from the usual sports."[3]

Special Orders No 29 Washington D.C. Feby 15th 1864

1 - Private A.W. Hyndman Co B, 50th N.Y.V.E. on duty as Clerk for Gen Court Martial is hereby returned to his regiment.

2 - Private H.M. Mathews Co. G. 50th N.Y.V.E. is hereby detailed as clerk for the Genl. Court Martial, now in session at Camp of 15th N.Y.V.E. and will report for duty immediately to Lieut Livingston A.D.C. Judge Advocate.

3 - Private John Fagan Co. D. 15th N.Y.V.E. is hereby detailed for duty as Clerk for the Genl. Court Martial now in session at Camp of 15th N.Y.V.E. and will report immediately to Lieut Livingston A.D.C. Judge Advocate.

On February 20 Owen wrote home that "there is little going on now save the old routine of camp duty which is always nearly the same, but when there is not too much of it, all goes well, as are the circumstances now."[4]

General Orders No 4 Washington Feby 21st 1864

There will be an inspection by Regiments of the different commands in this Brigade on Tuesday the 23rd inst. at 10 A.M. by the A.A. In. General. [Acting Assistant Inspector General]

Special Orders No 30 Washington D.C. Feby 1864

Some irregularity having existed in regard to passes for men to leave camp for short distances, the following will in future be the rules governing the issue of passes. Commandants of Companies may allow two or three men at one time to leave camp to visit in its immediate vicinity for not over two hours at any one time between Guard Mounting and retreat and not after the last named hour. but men so absent must always have the written pass of the commandant of their Company.

In fact, the above special order should have been published as a general order since it does not refer to an individual, but issues a command for the brigade as a whole. Both adjutants and adjutants' clerks were, even at this late date, somewhat novices to Army Regulations.

Special Orders No 31 Washington D.C. Feby 23rd. 1864

Private Seth F. Richardson Co B, 50th N.Y.V.E. on duty at these Hd. Qrs. is hereby returned to his regiment.

Special Orders No 32 Washington D.C. Feby 25th 1864

Musician James Prospheri is hereby appointed Band Master of the Engineer Brigade, to take effect from Feby 7th 1864

Although regimental bands had been disbanded in 1862, many brigades maintained their bands. According to Army Regulations, each band was to consist of 16 privates and a chief musician.

Special Orders No 33 Washington D.C. Feby 25th. 1864

Leave of Absence is granted to the following named Officer.
Captain John F. Caslow A.Q.M. for ten (10) days.

General Orders No 5 Washington D.C Feb 26th 1864

I. - Before a General Court Martial of which Major Wesley Brainard 50th N.Y.V. Engineers is President, convened at camp of the 15th N.Y.V.E. Washington D.C. by virtue of Special Orders No. 16 Par 2 from Head Quarters Engineer Brigade A - o - P. of January 23rd 1864, were arraigned and tried

1. - Private Nathan Hill Co. "G." 50th N.Y.V.E. on the following
Charge   Sleeping on Post
Finding   "Guilty."
Sentence: - To forfeit ten dollars per month of his monthly pay during the remainder of his term of enlistment and to be put at hard labor - with ball and chain weighing not less than fifteen pounds for thirty consecutive days (dating from the publication of this order), and when not at hard labor during said thirty days to be confined in the Brigade Guard house.

2. Private Timothy Hennessey Co. B. 15th N.Y.V.E. upon the following
Charge   Deserting his post
Finding   "Guilty"
Sentence - To forfeit ten dollars per month of his monthly pay for six months and to be subject to a course of Hydropathic treatment for six consecutive days after the publication of this order.

3. Private James McLaughlin Co B. 15th N.Y.V.E. upon the following
Charge   Desertion
Finding   "Guilty"
Sentence - To forfeit all pay that is or may become due him from the United States for the balance of his term of service, to make good the time he was absent from his regiment, without pay - to be placed at hard labor for sixty (60) days with ball and chain weighing not less than (24) twenty four pounds (said sixty days dating from the publication of this order) and to have a placard marked "for Desertion" placed upon his back, when at hard labor, and when not at hard labor during the sixty days to be confined in the Brigade Guard House

4 Floyd Moulton Musician Co. "B" 50th. Regt. N.Y.V.E. upon the following
Charge   Desertion
Finding   Not Guilty "but "Guilty" of absence without leave"
Sentence - To forfeit ten dollars per month of his monthly pay for four (4) months

5 Artificer Daniel Barns Co. B. 50th N.Y.V.E. upon the following.
Charge   Desertion
Finding   "Not Guilty" "but "Guilty" of "absence without leave"
      Sentence - To be reduced to the ranks as a second class private and in addition to the ($30) thirty dollars already charged for his apprehension to ten dollars ($10) per month of his monthly pay for four (4) months.

6 Private Charles Goodwin Co. B. 50th N.Y.V.E. upon the following
Charge   Desertion
Finding   "Not Guilty. "but Guilty" of "absence without leave"
Sentence - To forfeit in addition to the ($30) thirty dollars already paid for his apprehension, ten ($10) dollars of his monthly pay for (4) months and to be put at hard labor with a ball and chain, weighing not less than twelve (12) pounds for fifteen (15) days (dating from the publication of this order) and when not at such hard labor during such period to be confined in the Brigade Guard House.

7 Artificer George W. Canfield Co. "C." 50th N.Y.V.E. upon the following,
Charge   Desertion
Finding   "Not Guilty" "but "Guilty" of "absence without leave"
Sentence - To be reduced to the ranks as a second class private and in addition to the thirty ($30) dollars already charged to his apprehension to forfeit ten ($10) dollars per month of his monthly pay for four (4) months.

8 Private Patrick O'Driscoll Co "C" 50th Regt N.Y.V.E. upon the following
Charge 1st   Violation of the 46th Article of War
Specifications   In this that the said private Patrick O'Driscoll of Company and Regiment aforesaid, having been regularly posted as a Sentinel by a Corporal of the Guard, was found away from his post asleep
Charge 2nd   Drunkenness while on duty as a member of the Guard
Finding   Of the Specification of the 1st charge   "Guilty"
      Of 1st charge   "Guilty"
      Of 2nd charge   "Guilty"
Sentence - To forfeit ten ($10) dollars per month of his monthly pay for (5) five months, and to be paraded in front of the Guard House, inside a "Gabion" marked "for drunkenness on Duty" for hour hours each day for ten consecutive days (dating from the publication of this order)

9 Private Peter Bohan of Co. "C" 50th N.Y.V.E. upon the following
charge   Violation of the 46th Article of War.
Specification   In this that the said Private Peter Bohan of Company and Regiment aforesaid, having been regularly posted as a Sentinel by a Corporal of the Guard was found away from his post asleep.
Charge 2nd   Drunkenness while on duty as a member of the Guard

Finding   Of the Specification of the 1st Charge "Not Guilty"
Of the 1st charge   "Not Guilty"
Of the 2nd charge   "Not Guilty"
and the court does therefore acquit him the said private Peter Bohan.

I.I. The proceedings of the General Court Martial in the foregoing cases having been transmitted to the General Commanding Brigade, the following are the orders thereon.

The proceedings, findings and sentences in the cases of Private Hill Co. "G." Musician Floyd Moulton Co. "B" Private Patrick O'Driscoll Co "C" Private Peter Bohan Co. "C" of the 50th N.Y.V. Engrs. Private Timothy Hennessey Co "B." and Private James McLaughlin Co "B." 15th Regt N.Y.V.E. are approved. The comd'g officers of the Regiments to which they respectively belong will see that the sentences are carried into effect. Private Peter Bohan will be restored to duty.

Upon the recommendation of all the members of the Court as much of the sentences of Artificer Daniel Barnes Co "B" Private Elias Goodwin Co. "B." and Artificer George V. Canfield Co. "C" of the 50th N.Y.V. Engrs. as forfeits ($10) ten dollars per month of their monthly pay for four months is hereby remitted upon condition that said Barnes, Goodwin and Canfield shall not absent themselves without leave during the four months next ensuing the promulgation of their sentences. The remainder of their sentences will be carried into effect.

General Orders No. 6, Washington D.C. Feby 27th 1864

Commanding Officers of Regiments and Detachments of this Brigade, will muster their men for pay on the 29th inst.

General Orders No. 7 Washington D.C. Feby 29th 1864

I. Upon the recommendation of all the members of the Court, so much of the sentence of Musician Floyd Moulton Co. "B" 50th Regt. N.Y.V.E. as forfeits ten (10) dollars per month of his monthly pay for four months is hereby remitted upon condition that said Moulton shall not absent himself without leave during the four months next ensuing the publication of this order.

I.I. Before a General Court Martial of which Major Wesley Brainard 50th N.Y.V.E. is president - convened at the Camp of the 15th N.Y.V.E. Washington D.C. by virtue of Special Orders No 16 Par II.II from Head Quarters Engineer Brigade A-o-P of January 23rd. 1864, was arraigned and tried.

Artificer Hugh Keen Co. "D" 15th N.Y.V.E. upon the following.
Charge   Drunkenness on Post
Finding   "Not Guilty"
and the Court does therefore acquit said Artificer Hugh Keen Co. "D" 15th N.Y.V.E.

I.I.I. The proceedings in the case of Artificer Hugh Keen are approved and he will be immediately restored to duty.

In the camps, new men were drifting into the units, and thoughts turned to the upcoming campaign. Sergeant Owen wrote home on March 5: "We received ten recruits Thursday. Lester Champlin was among them, also Fred Hunt. I am afraid we will not fill the company up. It seems that most of the men that have enlisted for the company have been coaxed away. We have now 109 men in the company. The health of the company is very good. We are having fine times, and fine weather. I am engaged two hours each day drilling the recruits."

General Orders No. 8, Washington D.C. March 6th 1864

The Ponton drills of this command will be resumed at once. These will be a drill by successive Pontons on Monday, Wednesday & Friday mornings at the usual hours for drill (9 1/2 to 11 1/2) when as many of the old men can be spared from their other duties will be distributed among the recruits to assist in instructing them.

On Tuesday & Thursday at the usual hour (2 to 4) there will be ponton drill by battalion under the direction of a Field Officer of each regiment when practicable. - when the whole of each regiment will be out - except the Guard and such number of mechanics & as may appear to necessary to complete the barrack within the week.

The drills as infantry will be continued at the hours above named, whenever practicable without interfering with the ponton drills above directed and with as large a portion of each regiment out as can be spared from the fatigue duty required for arranging the barracks and drill grounds. The new recruits - being excused from this fatigue duty, will be drilled at least six hours a day - the hours other than those named above to be designated by the Regimental Commander.

Special Orders No 34, Washington D.C. March 10th 1864

The following named privates of the 15th & 50th N.Y.V.E. are hereby detailed for duty in the Brigade Hospital, until further orders.

John R. Hewilt Co B, 50th N.Y.V.E.   Milton Derby Co G, 50th N.Y.V.E.
Martin Bacon " " " " " "   Philip McFindly Co D, " " " " "
Henry Warren " C " " " " "   James Randall " B 15th N.Y.V.E.
Chas. A. Inquton " E " " " " "   Peter O'Donnell " B " " " " "

Special Orders No 35 Washington D.C. March 11th 1864

Leave of absence is granted to the following named officer.
Lieut Sidney Geo. Gynne Adjt 50th Regt. N.V.Y.E. for ten (10) days.

General Orders No. 9, Washington D.C. March 12th, 1864

The Brigade are hereby notified that the designation of this station is and it will be known hereafter in all official communications of the command as the "Engineer Depot ' and all other designations of this station or former encampment - will be avoided in such communications for the future.

Special Orders No 36 Washington D.C. March 14th. 1864

Leave of absence is granted to the following named Officers.
Lieut Jacob Haven Adjt 15th N.Y.V. Engrs. for ten (10) days
Lieut Charles F. Carroll, 50th N.Y.V.E. for (3) days.

Special Orders No 37 Washington D.C. March 16th. 1864

I. - Private Alonzo Randall Co. G. 50th. on duty in the Ambulance Corps of this command is hereby returned to his regiment.

I.I. - Private Geo. Woods Co. G. 50th N.Y.V.E. is hereby detailed for duty in the Ambulance Corps, and will report immediately to Lt Roosa for duty until further orders.

General Orders No. 10, Washington D.C. March 17th 1864

I. Before a General Court Martial of which Major Wesley Brainard 50th New York Vol Engineers is President, convened at the camp of the 15th N.Y.V.E. Washington D.C. by virtue of Special Orders No. 11, Par 2. from Head Quarters Engineer Brigade A-o-P. of Jan 23rd. were arraigned and tried.

1. Private Wm. Fairbanks Co. "A" 15th Regt. N.Y.V.E. on the following
Charge	"Drunkenness"
Finding	"Guilty"
Sentence	To be put at hard labor for thirty consecutive

days with a ball and chain weighing not less than twenty four pounds attached to his left leg and when not at such labor during said thirty days to be confined in the Brigade Guard House.

2. Private John S. Robinson Co. G. 50th N.Y.V.E. upon the following
Charge 1st	Desertion of Post
Charge 2nd	Absenting himself from Camp without leave from proper authority
Finding	Guilty of both charges
Sentence	To forfeit ten dollars per month of his

monthly pay for two months and to be put at hard labor for thirty days with a ball and chain weighing not less than twenty four pounds, and when not performing such labor during said thirty days to be confined in the Brigade Guard House.

3 Private Patrick Lynch Co. D. 15th N.Y.V.E. on the following
Charge	Conduct prejudicial to good order and Military Discipline"
Finding	"Guilty"
Sentence	- To forfeit ten dollars per month of his monthly

pay for two months to be placed at hard labor with a ball and chain weighing not less than twenty four pounds attached to his left leg, for twenty days, and when not at labor during said twenty days to be confined in the Brigade Guard House.

    4   Private John Daily Co. "D" 15th Regt. N.Y.V.E. on the following
Charge   Conduct prejudicial to good order and Military Discipline
Finding   "Guilty"
Sentence   To forfeit ten dollars per month of his monthly pay for two months, to be placed at hard labor with a ball and chain weighing not less than twenty four pounds attached to his left leg, for twenty days, and when not at labor during said twenty days, to be confined in the Brigade Guard House.

    5. Private Joseph H. Youngs Co. C. 50th Regt. N.Y.V.E. on the following

               Charge   Desertion
               Finding   "Not Guilty" but Guilty of absence without leave
               Sentence   To forfeit in addition to the $30 already paid for his apprehension ten dollars per month of his monthly pay for four months, and to be put at hard labor with a ball and chain weighing not less than twenty four pounds attached to his left leg for twenty days and when not at such hard labor to be confined in the Brigade Guard House.

    6   James Kennedy Private of Co "C." 50th N.Y.V.E. on the following
               Charge   Violation of the 46th Article of War
               Specification   In this that the said James Kennedy, private of Co. "C." 50th Regt. N.Y.V.E. having been regularly mounted as a member of the Engineer Brigade Guard and having been duly posted as a sentinel of said Guard was on or about the night of the 13th of July 1864 while a member of said Guard found asleep on his post.
               Finding   "Guilty"
               Sentence - To forfeit $10 per month of his monthly pay for six months, and to put at hard labor for thirty days with a ball and chain weighing not less than 24 pounds, attached to his left leg and when not at such hard labor during said thirty days to be confined in the Brigade Guard House.

    7   Private Patrick Dunn Co. "D" 15th N.Y.V.E. on the following.
               Charge   Conduct prejudicial to good order and Military Discipline
               Specification   In that the said Private Dunn a private of Co. "D" 15th N.Y.V.E. having been regularly mounted by the staff officer of the day of the Brigade Guard on the morning of the 2nd. of January 1864, when called on to go on post with the relief to which he was assigned, was found to be drunk as to totally unfit him for Guard, or any other Military Duty all this at Washington D.C on or about the 2nd. day of Feby 1864

Finding   "Guilty"
Sentence   To be placed at hard labor for thirty days with a ball and chain weighing not less than 24 pounds attached to his left leg, and when not at such labor during said thirty days to be confined in the Brigade Guard House.

8 Private Stephen G. Doxey Co. "a." 15th N.Y.V.E. on the following
Charge   Desertion
Finding   "Guilty"
Sentence   To be dishonorably discharged [from] the service of the united States, to be marked with a letter "D" one inch in length in indelible ink, on his left hip as a deserter and a letter "D" of the same length in indelible ink on his right hip as confirmed and worthless drunkard, to have one side of his head shaved, and the buttons of his uniform and other Military insignia, stripped from him, and to be drummed out of Camp in presence of his regiment, at such time and place as the Commanding General may direct.

I.I. The proceedings of the General Court Martial in the foregoing cases having been transmitted to the General Commanding Brigade the following are the orders thereon.

The proceedings findings and sentences in the cases of Private Wm. Fairbanks Co. "A" Private Patrick Lynch Co. D" Private John Daily Co. "D" Private Patrick Dunn Co. "D" Private Stephen G. Doxey Co. "A," of the 15th N.Y.V.E. Private John S. Robinson Co. "G" Private James Kennedy Co. "C" of the 50th N.Y.V.E. are approved. The commanding officers of the Regiment to which they respectively belong will see that the sentences are carried into effect immediately on the publication of these orders. The sentence of Stephen G. Doxey Co. "A" 15th N.Y.V.E. will be carried into effect at the first "dress parade" after such publication.

Upon recommendation of all the members of the Court, so much of the sentence of Private Joseph H. Youngs of Co "C". 50th Regt N.Y.V.E. as forfeits ten ($10) dollars per month of his monthly pay for four months is hereby remitted, upon condition that said private Youngs shall not absent himself without leave during the four months next ensuing the promulgation of his sentence. The remainder of his sentence will be carried into effect.

General Orders No. 11, Washington DC. March 17th 1864

Lieut F.W. Pettes 50th Regt. N.Y.V.E. arrested for disobedience of orders from these headquarters and neglect of duty in relation to the drills of his regiment, upon his acknowledgment of his error. - and the explanation offered by him is hereby released from arrest and restored to duty.

In passing over, without further action, this neglect of duty, but a single instance of many that have occurred lately in reference to the drills of these regiments the Commanding General does not think it can be necessary to remind the officers of this command that all orders must be implicitly obeyed, both as to the manner, and to the time of execution. That any who takes upon himself to judge of and vary from the orders given. - without the previous sanction of the commander - is guilty of a high military offense - and will be undeserving of being confided in for any important military duty - and while the offer, in a proper manner of any information, which might modify an order - is not objected to - still a change of an order - without such sanction - except in extraordinary emergencies, in which the officers must take this risk of being justified - is not -and cannot be considered as any thing less excusable than a willful disobedience of orders which should bring a severe punishment.

Special Orders No 38, Washington D.C. March 17th. 1864

In the case of Augustus Peabody private Co. C. 15th Regt. N.Y.V.E. in the opinion of the General Commanding, requiring immediately example, the General Court Martial now in session at the Camp of the 15th Regt. N.Y.V.E. is hereby directed to extend its session on the 21st day of March 1864, until the hour of 5 P.M.

The ranks continued to fill. On March 20, Sergeant Owen wrote home: "Well, we are still here and things go on about the same. Yesterday we received eleven new recruits. The company now contains 120 men, thirty more, and then..... We feel confident that the company will be filled up."[5]

Special Orders No 39 Washington March 22nd. 1864

Capt M.H. McGarth 50th N.Y.V.E. having completed the duty for which he was detailed by S.O. No. 3 Jany 3rd. 1864 from these Head Qrs. is hereby ordered to report to the Commanding Officer of his Regiment for duty.

General Orders No. 12 Washington D.C. March 21st 1864

The monthly inspection of the A.A. Ins. Genl. will take place on the 24th inst. at 10 A.M. The command will be inspected by regiments. Officers of new Companies will be instructed in the form of Report to be made to the Inspecting Officer. - Company reports will be furnished immediately after Inspection.

Special Orders No 40 Washington March 22nd. 1864

Private Geo. M. Gosman Co. B. 15th Regt. N.Y.V.E. is hereby detailed for duty as guard at these Head Quarters until further orders.

Special Orders No 41 Washington D.C. March 25th. 1864

I Private B. Rogers Co. D. 15th N.Y.V.E. acting as clerk of the General Court Martial now in session at the camp of the 15th N.Y.V.E. is hereby returned to his regiment.

I.I. - Martin McNamara Private Co. C. 15th N.Y.V.E. is hereby detailed for duty as clerk of the General Court Martial, in place of Rogers returned to his regiment.

Special Orders No. 42 Washington D.C. March 26th 1864

The following named privates of the 50th N.Y.V.E. are hereby detailed for duty in the Brigade Hospital, until further orders.

Henry J. Bruikeshand	Co. "C."
Wm. A. Tomer	" "A.":
E.A. Dunkham	" "D."

On March 28 the Army of the Potomac's assistant adjutant general wrote General Benham: "The commanding general directs that the Fiftieth New York Engineers join the engineer camp near Rappahannock Station, with as little delay as practicable. If there are men in this regiment that you think it necessary to detail for special service at the depot you are authorized to retain such men."[6] Benham immediately issued the following:

Special Orders No. 43 Washington March 29th 1864

I. - Col Pettes will proceed on the 30th inst with companies B, C, D, L, & M of the 50th N.Y.V.Engineers, by rail to the Camp of the Ponton Detachment near Rappahannock Station Va. He will report on arrival by telegraph to the Hd. Qrs. of the Army of the Potomac. The men will be provided with one days cooked rations. Lieut. Roosa will send with the Regt. his Ambulance Sergeant with two ambulances & medicine wagon with their horses, drivers & equipments

The Brigade Qr Mr will provide transportation.

Asst Surgeon Beers will remain in charge of the sick of the 50th Regiment Major Brainerd & Capts Pasonius & Schenck will remain at this Depot, until relieved from the Court Martial now in session.

I.I. - Lieut Carroll is hereby relieved from duty at the Workshops and will take charge of Co. "G." until Capt. Personius reports to this regiment when Lieut Carroll wil return to this Depot.

I.I.I. - The following named privates of the 50th N.Y.V.E. on duty in the Qr Mr Dept. of this command are hereby returned to their Regiment

| Henry Mallette Otis Thayer | Morgan R. Cleveland |
| W.H. Remington | Nathan Moore V Moore & N.F. Wheeler |

IV. The following named non-commissioned Officers and privates of the 50th N.Y.V.E. are hereby detailed for duty in the Engineer Workshops, and will report imediately to Capt Geo. W. Ford.

Private Frederick Hank Co. C.	Private M.J. Stuart Co. G.
" Tufts " "	Sergt - Sweet " H.
" Owin S. Crandell " "	Artif. Henry McGlackin Co. H.
" Julius Allen " "	" Wm. A. Salsbury " "
" C.H. Wutterman " "	" Thomas Harris " I

Corpl. Smith " D	" Mortimer Searls " "
Private Gideon Chilson " "	Private R.F. Rugg" D
Sergt H.De Wakiman " F.	" H.L. Dickins " G
Priv. J.M. Murphey " G.	" J.H. Perry " "
" J. Vail " "	

Finally, on March 30, the campaign, at least as far as the brigade was concerned, began. In it, the 50th was to be divided into three battalions, each one assigned to a corps in the Army of the Potomac, with its main duty providing road building and bridging support. The First Battalion under Major Wesley Brainerd accompanied the II Corps; Major Edmund O. Beers' Second Battalion was with the VI Corps, and the Third Battalion of soon-to-be Major George W. Ford with the V Corps. Each battalion would have a train of boats and equipment capable of crossing 300 feet of water. The 15th, only at battalion strength of five companies, would also see duty with the Engineer Brigade directly under Army of the Potomac headquarters. As well Lieutenant Colonel Ira Spaulding, of the 50th, would command a reserve battalion made up of nine companies of the 50th with two trains of canvas pontoon bridging boats and equipment, directly.

Special Orders No. 44 Washington March 31st. 1864

The cases before the General Court Martial now in session at the camp of the 15th N.Y.V.E. in the opinion of the General Commanding requiring immediate example said court is hereby directed to extend its sessions on the 31st March 1st, 2nd, & 4th. of April until the hour of 5 P.M.

Special Orders No. 45 Washington D.C. April 3rd. 1864

I. Corporal Peter Cody 15th. N.Y.V.E. on duty at this Hd. Qrs. is hereby returned to his regiment

I.I. - Corporal J. Rosenthal Co. "A," 15th N.Y.V.E. is hereby detailed for duty as guard at these Hd. Qrs. until further orders.

I.I.I. -- Sergt Tobias Wilmer Co F, 50th N.Y.V.E. is hereby detailed as Draughtsman at these Head Quarters, and will report for duty as soon as possible.

Special Orders No. 46 Washington D.C. April 5th 1864

Capt John F. Caslow A.Q.M. Engineer Brigade is hereby ordered to proceed with Clerk, Wagon Master and Orderly to the Camp of the 50th N.Y.V.E. near Rappahannock Station, Va. on business.

Having completed his business, Capt Caslow will return immediately to this depot.

Special Orders No. 47 Washington D.C. April 9th. 1864

Sergt. Wm. E. Bennett and privates Gray and Butler 50th N.Y.V. Engineers are hereby ordered to take charge of a ponton train of six boats and wagons, and two chess wagons to go by Rail to Cumberland

Md. On arrival, Sergt. Bennett will turn over said train to Lt. Jno. R. Meigs of the Engineer Corps taking his receipts for the same, after making whatever explanation may be necessary. Sergt. Bennett & privates Gray & Butler will return without delay to this camp.

Special Orders No. 48 Washington D.C. April 11th 1864

Corporal Buck and one private 50th N.Y.V. Engrs. are hereby ordered to take charge of a ponton train of six ponton wagons and go by rail to Cumberland Md. On arrival Corpl. Buck will turn over said train to Lieut Jno. R. Meigs of the Engineer Corps taking his receipts for the same, when he will return without delay to this camp.

Special Orders No. 49 Washington D.C. April 9th. 1864

The General Court Martial convened by Special Orders No. 16 from these Head Quarters, having on the 8th day of April 1864 adjourned sine die is this day reconviened for the purpose of transacting such further business as may be brought before it.

Special Orders No. 50 Washington D.C. April 14th 1864

Asst Surgeon Beers 50th N.Y.V. Engineers now in charge of the sick of this regiment at this depot will immediately turn over his sick to Surgeon T. Z. Gibbs 15th N.Y.V.E. and will himself report to-morrow to the Head Qrs of this Regt at Rappahannock Station Va.

General Orders No. 13, Washington D.C. April 17th 1864

I. Before a General Court Martial of which Major Wesley Brainard 50th N.Y.V. Engrs. is President, commenced at the camp of the 15th N.Y.V.E. Washington D.C. by virtue of Special Orders No 16 Par 2 from Head Quarters Engineer Brigade A-o-P of Jan'y 23rd 1864 were arraigned and tried

1 Private Thomas O'Reilly Co. "D." 15th Regt. N.Y.V. Engineers upon the following

Charge	Absence without leave
Finding	Guilty
Sentence	To forfeit ten dollars per month of his

monthly pay for six months and to be put at hard labor for thirty days, with a ball and chain weighing not less than twenty four pounds attached to his left leg, and when not at such labor during said 30 days to be confined in the Brigade Guard House.

2 Artificer William Saunders Co "D" 15th N.Y. Vol. Engrs. upon the following

Charge 1st	Absence without leave
" 2nd	Conduct to the prejudice of good order & Military Discipline
Finding	Guilty
Sentence	To be reduced to 2nd. class private to be put

at hard labor for thirty days with a ball and chain weighing not less than twenty five pounds attached to his left leg and when not at such labor during said thirty days to be confined in the Brigade Guard House and to publicly ask pardon of the Officer offended, in the presence of his Regiment.

    3 Private Walter S. Fuller Co. "C" 50th Regt. N.Y.V.E. upon the following

Charge	Absence without leave
Findings	Not Guilty

and the court does therefore acquit him.

    4 Private John Gallagher Co. "C." 15th Regt. N.Y.V. Engrs. upon the following

Charge	Conduct to the prejudice of good order and military discipline
Finding	Guilty
Sentence	To forfeit $10 per month of his monthly pay

for eight months and to be put at hard labor for 60 days with a ball and chain weighing not less than twenty four pounds attached to his left leg and when not at such labor during said 60 days to be confined in the Brigade Guard House

    5 Private John Baldwin Co. C. 50th N.Y.V. Engrs. upon the following

Charge	Conduct prejudicial to good order and military discipline
Finding	Guilty
Sentence	To forfeit ten dollars per month of his

monthly pay for two months: and to be put at hard labor for twenty days, with a ball and chain weighing not less than twenty four pounds attached to his left leg, and while not at such labor during said twenty days, to be confined in the Brigade Guard House

    6 Private John Dale Co. d. 50th Regt. N.Y.V.E. upon the following

Charge	Conduct prejudicial to good order and military discipline
Finding	Guilty
Sentence	To forfeit ten dollars per month of his

monthly pay for four months, and to be put at hard labor for sixty (60) days with a ball and chain weighing not less than twenty four pounds attached to his left leg, and when not at such labor during said sixty days to be confined in the Brigade Guard House.

    7 Private Edward Shannon Co D. 50th N.Y.V.E. upon the following

Charge	Conduct prejudicial to good and military discipline
Finding	Guilty
Sentence	To forfeit ten dollars per month of his

monthly pay for four months, to be placed at hard labor for thirty days, with a ball and chain weighing not less than twenty four pounds attached to his left [leg], and when not at such hard labor, during said thirty days, to be confined in the Brigade Guard House.

8 Private Thomas Germain Co. A. 15th N.Y.V.E. upon the following

Charge	Desertion
Finding	Guilty
Sentence	To forfeit all pay and bounty due or hereaf-

ter to become due him from the United States.

9 Private James Printz Co. "D" 50th Regt. N.Y.V.E. upon the following

Charge	Conduct prejudicial to good order and military discipline
Finding	Not Guilty

and the court does therefore acquit him.

10 Private Francis L. McCarthy Co. A. 15th N.Y.V.E. upon the following

Charge	Desertion
Finding	Guilty
Sentence	In addition to the period for which he was

originally enlisted, to make good the time lost by his absence viz - from the twentieth day of June 1863 to the twenty ninth day of February 1864, and that without pay, to be put at hard labor for sixty days with a ball and chain weighing not less than twenty four pounds attached to his left leg and while not at such labor during said sixty days to be confined in the Brigade Guard House.

11 Christopher W. Walsh Private Co. A. 15th N.Y.V.E. upon the following

Charge	Desertion
Finding	Not Guilty - but Guilty of absence without leave
Sentence	To be put at hard labor for thirty days with a

ball and chain weighing not less than twenty four pounds attached to his left leg, and when not at such hard labor during said thirty days to be confined in the Brigade Guard House.

I.I - The proceedings of the General Court Martial in the above cases having been submitted to the General Commanding Brigade, the following are the orders thereon.

The proceedings findings and sentences in the cases of Private Thomas O'Reilly Co. "d." John Gallagher Co. "C." Thomas Germain Co. "A" Francis L. McCarthy Co. "A" Christopher W. Walsh Co. "A" Artificer Wm. Saunders Co. "D" of the 15th N.Y.V.E. Privates John Baldwin Co. 'C" John Dole Co 'D" Edward Shannon Co. D. of the [50th] N.Y.V. Engineers are approved. The Comd. Officers of the Regiments to which they belong will see that the sentences are carried into effect.

The proceedings & findings in the cases of Wallace S. Fuller Co. "C" James Printz Co. 'D' of the 50th N.Y.V.E. are approved and these men will be immediately returned to duty.

General Orders No. 14 Washington D.C. April 20th 1864

The usual monthly inspection by the A.A. In. Genl. of this command will take place on Friday April 22nd commencing at 10 A.M. The men are to carry their shelter tents on their knapsacks. Efforts will be made to supply all deficiencies that may now exist, before that time.

Shelter tents were pieces of white canvas, some 5 feet 2 inches by 4 feet 8 inches in size with a single row of buttons and button holes on three sides and a pair of holes for stake loops in each corner. Two, one carried by each soldier, could be buttoned to make a small shelter tent.

Special Orders No. 51 Washington D.C. April 23rd. 1864

The following named Non-commissioned Officers, Artificers, and privates of the 50th N.Y.V.E. are hereby detailed for duty with the Ambulance Corps of this command, until further orders.
Sergt Jos. Howard Co E, to take charge of ambulances &c in the 6th Corps.
" Mahlan Bumbridge Co G. " " " " " " " " 2nd. "
" John Chatterton " " " " " " " " " " 5th "

Private Henry J. farren Co H.	Private Parley Burton Co. M.
" James Willson " "	" W.H. Love " "
" Charles Sorder " B.	Chas. O. Howard " E.
" Edward Blanchard " G.	Edward Auhillis " L.
" James A. Boyce " C.	Daniel Snyder " L.
" Milton Turner " F.	Frank Van Hatten " K.
" Oliver Osborn " F.	Lewis Corborn " D.

If any of the above men are not found qualified for the position, Surgeon Hewitt is authorized to exchange them for others.

On April 23 Owen, who learned that he had been commissioned a second lieutenant in his regiment on March 17, wrote home that his men were "making preparations for the coming contest, which at the longest cannot be postponed much longer. Some of the detachments have joined their respective corps. Company I is building a stockade at Warrenton Junction which shows that this line of communication is to [be] kept. Captain Folwell, with part of the company, has been there two days, and in the morning, the rest of the company goes there to help complete the work. I am going and will take command which the captain is absent, as he has other matters to attend to here about trains, etc."[7]

General Orders No. 15 Washington April 25th 1864

Capt Alex Hull A.Q.M. having been assigned to duty as Qr Mr of this command by orders from Head Qrs of the Army will be obeyed and respected as such.

Capt. Jno J. Basoy having been relieved from duty here will turn over the Qr Mr property for which he is responsible to Capt Hull.

Special Orders No. 52 Washington D.C. April 25th. 1864

The following named non-com. officer and privates of the 15th N.Y.V.E. are hereby detailed for duty in the Ambulance Corps of this Brigade, and will report to Lieut J.L. Roosa, as soon as possible.

Sergt John Seaman Co C, 15th.　Priv Wm. Bennett Co C.
Priv Wm Buckbee " C "　　　　" Benj O'Donalds " B
" Wm. Quackenbush " A "　　" Saml. Brown " E.
" David Pratt " A "

General Orders No. 16 Washington April 26th. 1864

The sentences of the Court Martial in the cases of privates Grey and Cusick of the 15th Regt. N.Y.V.E. having been approved by the Commanding General of this Army, the General commanding this Brigade is directed to see their sentences executed.

The sentences of said private Grey being for desertion a second time "to be shot to death by musketry at such time and place as the commanding General may direct"

And the Commanding General having directed that these executions should take place upon Friday the 29th. of April inst; and after 12 Meridian of that day, it is hereby ordered that said sentences shall be executed upon the above named prisoners upon the day ordered the 29th inst or as near the hour of 4 1/2 P.M. as practicable

The officers and men of this brigade present at this depot available for duty except the necessary guards, will be formed for the occasion in one battalion at about 3 1/2 P.M. to be present as directed at the execution, which will take place on the Eastern edge of the Brigade parade between 14th & 15th Streets East.

The necessary details for the formation of the troops, details for escort and execution will be under immediate direction of Col W.H. Pettes 50th N.Y.V.E.

Lieut O'Keiffe 15th N.Y.V.E. will act as provost Marshal on this occasion.

These sentences were, for some reason, not carried out. The names Grey and Cusick do not appear in the U.S. Army's official *List of U.S. Soldiers Executed by United States Military Authorities during The Late War.* Not one individual attributed to either the 15th or 50th New York Engineers appears on this list.

On April 26 Benham was advised that "General Burnside has been authorized to call on you for a bridge in case he requires one to replace the one of ten boats now laid across the Rappahannock. You will answer his requisition and furnish the necessary detail from your command to superintend the laying of the bridge and taking the proper care of it."[8]

General Orders No. 17 Washington D.C. April 28. 1864

Commanding officers of Regiments and Detachments of this Brigade will muster their [commands] for pay on the 30th. inst.

General Orders No. 18 April 29th 1864

I Before a General Court Martial of which Major Wesley Brainerd 50th N.Y.V.E. is President, convened at the camp of the 15th N.Y.V.E. Washington D.C. by virtue of Special Orders No. 11 Par 2 from Head Quarters Engineer Brigade A-o-P of January 23rd 1864, were arraigned and tried.

1 - Private James M. Miller Co. A. 50th N.Y.V.E. upon the following
Charge 1st Desertion
Charge 2nd - Absence without leave
Charge 3rd - Drunkenness
Finding - Of the 1st. charge - Not Guilty but Guilty of absence without leave - Of the 2nd Charge Guilty - of the 3rd Charge - Guilty
Sentence - To forfeit in addition to the $30 already paid for his apprehension, his monthly pay for four months and to be put at hard labor for thirty days with a ball and chain weighing not less than twenty four pounds, attached to his left leg, and when not at such labor - during said thirty days to be confined in the Brigade Guard House, and to be subjected to a Hydropathic plunge in the Eastern Branch of the Potomac between the hours of 7 & 8 A.M. once a day for ten alternate days.

2 - Private Peter Wilmet - Co B. 15th N.Y.V.E. upon the following.
Charge - Desertion
Finding - Guilty
Sentence - To forfeit one years pay, to make good the time lost by desertion, and to be placed, at hard labor for sixty days, with a ball and chain weighing not less than 24 lbs attached to his left leg, and when not at such labor during said sixty days to be placed in confinement.

3 - Private Dennis B. Knapp Co. M. 50th N.Y.V.E. upon the following
Charge - Desertion
Finding - Not Guilty
and the Court does therefore acquit him

4 - Private James Foster 2nd Regt N.Y.V.E. upon the following
Charge Desertion
Finding Guilty
Sentence - To make good the time lost by desertion without pay, and in addition to forfeit ten ($10) per month of his monthly pay for six months and to be put at hard labor for sixty days with a ball and chain weighing not less than 24 pounds attached to his left leg, and when not at such hard labor during said sixty day to be confined in the Brigade Guard House.

5 Private Cornelius Horrigan Co C. 15th N.Y.V.E. upon the following
Charge - Conduct prejudicial to good order and military discipline

Finding - Guilty

Sentence - To forfeit his monthly pay for the period of one month, to be put at hard labor for 30 days with a ball and chain weighing not less than 24 pounds attached to his left leg, and when not at such labor during said 30 days to be placed in confinement, and to apologize to his comrade for his offense in the presence of his regiment.

6 Private Bernard Glasbie 2nd Regt. N.Y.V. Engrs upon the following

Charge -   Desertion

Finding   Guilty

Sentence   To forfeit all pay and bounty now due him from the United States, and to make good the time lost by his desertion without pay.

7 - Private Timothy Cronin Co D 15th N.Y.V.E. upon the following

Charge 1st. - Offering violence to his superior officer, he being in the execution of his office

Charge 2nd. - Conduct to the prejudice of good order and military discipline

Finding -   Guilty of both charges

Sentence -   To ask pardon of his superior officer - Sergeant Doran, publicly and before his regiment, to forfeit his monthly pay for the period of six months, to be put at hard labor with a ball and chain weighing not less than 24 pounds attached to his left leg for the period of 90 days and when not at such labor during said 90 days to be placed in confinement.

8 - Private Mathew Lee - Co. B. 15th N.Y.V.E. upon the following

Charge -   Desertion

Finding -   Not Guilty

and the Court does therefore acquit him.

I.I - The proceedings in the above cases having been submitted to the General Commanding the Brigade, the following are the orders thereon.

The proceedings, findings and sentences in the cases of Private James M. Miller Co. A. 50th N.Y.V.E. - Peter Wilmot - Co B - Cornealius Horrigan Co C. - Timothy Cronin Co D. 15th N.Y.V.E. - Private James Foster 2nd Regt N.Y.V.E. now Co D of the 15th N.Y.V.E. are approved. The Comdg Officers of the Regiments to which they respectively belong will see that the sentences are carried into execution

The Proceedings and findings in the cases of Mathew Lee Co . 15th and Dennis B. Knapp Co M. 50th N.Y.V.E. are approved and these men will be restored to duty.

I-I-I - There being no more business to bring before the court, said Court is hereby dissolved.

On April 30 Lieutenant Owen reported: "The headquarters with the regiment joined us on Wednesday last, the 30th. There are ten companies here now. Company A is in Washington and E is at Hazel Run, making twelve in all, all of which are full except two, and they nearly."[9]

CHAPTER 4
From the Wilderness to City Point: May 1864

▶────────────────◀

On May 1 Ambrose Burnside directed Benham to send a pontoon train to Rappahannock Station to be ready to be built across the river there by the third.[1]

Special Orders No. 53 Washington D.C. May 2nd. 1864

I. - Artificer Charles S. Baldwin Co B, 15th N.Y.V.E. on duty as Guard at these Head Quarters, having been promoted to Corporal, is hereby returned to his regiment.

I.I. - Artificer Daniel R. Ganeltson Co B, 15th N.Y.V.E. is hereby detailed for duty as Guard at these Head Quarters until further orders.

On the second, Benham had a pontoon bridge train loaded onto railroad cars and sent off around one in the afternoon, under command of Captain H.V. Slosson, Co. D, 15th New York, a 75-man-strong company. Slosson was directed to turn the completed bridge over to the command of Captain McDonald of the V Corps and retain Burnside's bridge under a "selected guard of pontoniers" selected from his company.[2] Slosson arrived on time, getting the bridge ready for use by 11 on the morning of the third.[3]

Others of the brigade were also on the move. On May 4 Lieutenant Owen's company bridged the Rapidan at Ely's Ford at daylight. After most of the II Corps had gotten over the bridge, the men reloaded their pontoons and went on, camping that night at Chancellorsville.

"The 5th, the fight began," Owen wrote home.

We went nearly to the front on the left with our train but came back faster than we went to Chancellorsville where we left the train and went the same night with arms and ammunition to the front. Reported to General Warren, Commanding 2d Corps.

On the morning of the 6th at daylight, we went into the line of battle, front of the old Wilderness Tavern, where we remained twenty-four

54

hours in rifle pits back of the first line of battle. There were no casualties in Company I. One man of Company E was hit with a piece of shell in the head, did not kill him. The fighting raged in front of us all day. We had a good position which we made better in the day by throwing up rifle pits, etc.[4]

Special Orders No. 54 Washington D.C. May 6th 1864

I. - A Court of Inquiry having been asked by Lieut A. H. Megary 15th N.Y.V.E. to investigate the circumstances attending the shooting of Private Owen Campbell 15th N.Y.V.E. by him, the following named officers are hereby appointed [to] such court.

Col W.H. Pettes	50th N.Y.V.E.
Major W.A. Ketchum	15th " " " "
Capt T. Lubey	15th " " " "
Capt Stephen Chester	15th Recorder

Said Court will assemble in the barracks at 10 A.M. on the 7th. inst and in addition to the investigation of the circumstances, the court will express its opinion as to the necessity for the act.

I.I. - Major Geo. W. Ford 50th N.Y.V. Engineers is hereby relieved from the command of the Workshops at this Depot and will report as soon as practicable to his detachment in the field.

Major Ford will turn over to Capt J.L. Robbins 50th N.Y.V.E. all the Engineer and other property for which he is responsible and Capt Robbins is hereby assigned to the command vacated by Major Ford.

I.I.I. - Col W.H. Pettes the senior officer of the 50th Regt present at this Depot will have charge in future of all purchases of property and of all disbusements on account of the Workshops.

On May 7 Owen's company returned to II Corps headquarters where they rested during the day, going back to Chancellorsville that night. On the eighth they headed towards the Spotsylvania Court House, going to the Ny River on the tenth where they camped until the evening of the twelfth, when they moved to Zoan Church, some four miles from Fredericksburg.

Meanwhile, Slosson and his company, receiving no orders one way or another and lacking transportation, remained on the Rappahannock as late as May 9.

General Orders No. 19 Washington D.C. May 9th. 1864

Until further orders the calls for the different duties of this command will be sounded as follows.

Reveille	5 A.M.	Dinner	12 M
Police	5 1/2 " "	Drill	3 to 5 P.M.
Breakfast	6 " "	Recruit Drill	3 to 6 " "
Sick Call	6 1/2/ " "	Dress Parade	6 " "
Recruit Drill	6 1/2 to 7 1/2	Supper	6 1/2 " "
Guard Mounting	8	Tattoo	8 1/2 " "
Drill	8 1/2 to 10 1/2	Taps	9 " "

In the meantime, the entire Army of the Potomac opened its final campaign, heading across the Rapidan River and heading into the tangled area known as the Wilderness. At the same time, the Army of the James, under political appointee Major General Benjamin Butler, was under way to the Peninsula, not far from where McClellan had met so much grief two years earlier. The next day, the Federals marching into the Wilderness clashed with Lee's troops, hurriedly sent to fight in the brush and trees where the overwhelming Federal numbers would count for less than on open ground. While their fighting was going on, Butler's troops landed at City Point, now Hopewell.

Casualties in the Wilderness were heavy, with almost 17,700 dead, wounded, or missing. Grant sent back to Washington for reinforcements. Then, on the morning of May 7, he sent his army south, not north as so many stalemated Union generals had done before, towards Spotsylvania Court House. Lee quickly realized what the Army of the Potomac was up to and reacted by racing his troops towards that vital position.

In this move, six companies of the 50th, under Lieutenant Colonel Spaulding, acting as infantry assigned to the V Corps, were posted to the left of the 2nd Brigade, 1st Division, V Corps, just south of the Orange Turnpike. The rest of the regiment was scattered between that post and Washington, where some of its members still worked in the Engineer Depot. Some 350 officers and men of the Battalion of U.S. Engineers, under Captain George H. Mendell, were nearby, between two brigades of the 1st Division, V Corps, just north of the turnpike. Although they built temporary field fortifications, essentially, they, like the New Yorkers, had been assigned an infantry combat role in the fighting to come.[5]

On May 9 Edwin Stanton, Secretary of War, ordered Benham directly to built a pontoon bridge across the Rappahannock River opposite Fredericksburg.[6] According to Benham, he quickly produced a schedule of the transportation required for such a bridge. On May 10 all arrangements had been made and the bridging material was shipped off down the Potomac River, with the idea of them reaching the landing facilities at Aquia Creek before midnight. However, Benham was concerned since this operation was to take one of his four companies, while Company D was languishing without orders near Fredericksburg.[7]

And well he should have been concerned, for on May 11 came orders from the army's chief of staff, Major General Henry Halleck, to set up floating wharves at Belle Plain, in Virginia, by using surplus pontoons for the wharves, with barges for the wharf heads. Grant's army desperately needed supplies that could be more quickly brought by sea than overland, and these make-shift wharves would help meet that need. At ten in the morning of the eleventh, Captain Timothy Lubey and his men arrived at Belle Plain and began building a bridge from the shore to enable the unit to run the barges alongside to unload. Because the banks sloped so gently into the river there, Lubey found that he had to build out some 300 feet from shore to get into water deep enough to bring barges alongside to unload. Even then, steamers would not be able to be unloaded directly, and their cargoes would have to be unloaded into barges, which would then be towed to the make-shift wharves for unloading. The hundreds of sick and wounded straggling back from Grant's tremendous assaults clogged the roads and area around Belle Plain, adding to Captain Lubey's problems.[8]

Still, by one in the morning, working through the night by the dim lights available, the engineers under Captain Lubey were able to throw up a float-ing dock some 360 feet long.[9]

General Orders No. 20 Washington D.C. May 12th 1864

The Commanding General directs that no pedlars of any descrip-tion be admitted within the limits of the Camp.

Because the army did not supply many items needed both for comfort and necessity to its men, each regiment was authorized one sutler, a civil-ian trader who brought a stock of such items as canned food, clothing, and cleaning materials. A.H. Tower was the assigned sutler to the 50th, while the 15th had two sutlers over the course of its life, W.H. Cunningham and D.R. Smith.[10] These sutlers had monopolies on trade with their units and were usually believed to charge more money than their stock was worth. The men took every chance they could get to get something out of them for free. One infantryman recalled his regiment "discovered a sutler estab-lished near, went through him just to kill time. In other words, they upset his tent, which consisted of bread, apples, etc."[11]

Whenever troops came into an area, however, locals took advantage of the number of people with money nearby by bringing whatever they had to sell into camp, acting as independent peddlers. One infantryman recalled when his regiment finally received its pay: "Scarcely had the money got into the hands of those who had so hardly earned it before there was a grand entree of peddlers by the hundred. It was really amusing to see these vend-ers of wares of every description throng around every nook and corner of the camp. Some of those traveling sutlers having the rightful impression that 'a drop of the cure now and then would be handy in the house you know,' brought a quantity of dark green bottles with a suspicious look, and found ready customers in great abundance without any advertising what-ever, excepting a sly wink."[12]

Given this kind of disruption of camp discipline, most commanders tried to ban peddlers at one time or another. This had mixed results, as one infantryman recalled: "The boys have a good time, as they have orders to keep order, and confiscate all the goods of basket peddlers who come on the premises, and can keep the articles themselves."[13]

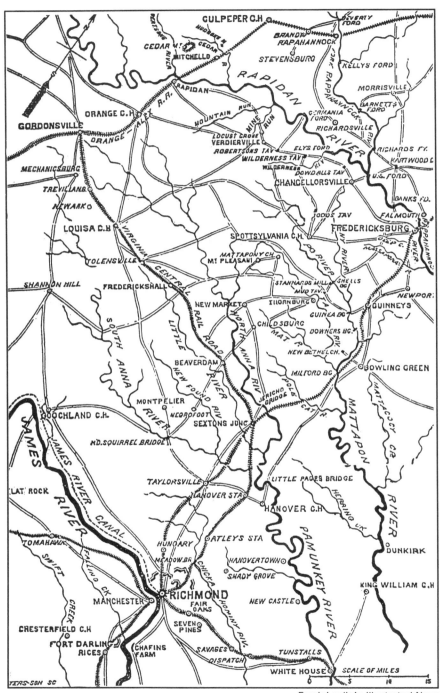

Frank Leslie's Illustrated News

On May 13 Benham was ordered to bring down all the remaining men of the brigade to Belle Plain to built and repair roads between there and Fredericksburg. The brigade was to bring some of its bridge train to build more floating wharves to facilitate the loading of stores and embarkation of the wounded. Only enough men needed to guard equipment at the Engineer Depot were to be left behind. The men at Fredericksburg were to report to the commander of the II Corps of the Army of the Potomac, while the bridge they built across the Rappahannock was to remain in place. Unfortunately, Slosson hadn't been told these new orders, instead being told to go back to Washington. Arranging transportation, his company arrived there by noon on the thirteenth, just in time to join the entire Brigade's move south.[14]

As Benham's men prepared to move, Lubey had problems of his own. He telegraphed back to Benham at Washington on May 13: "Please send me immediately axes, shovels, picks, and carpenters' tools. The quartermaster's department wants another dock made, but I have no pontoons or material to built it. Can you send me some? I should also like, if possible, more men, as my detail is too small to do half the work that is to be done. I do my best, and the men work night and day."[15]

Special Orders No. 55 Washington D.C. May 14th. 1864

Private George Uneber Co "C" 15th N.Y.V.E. is hereby detailed for duty in the Commissary Dept of this command until further orders, and will report immediately to Lieut Geo. W. Nares.

Benham's brigade marched to the wharf at the end of Sixth Street, in Washington, where they boarded boats heading for Belle Plain. They arrived there on the afternoon of the fifteenth, joining Lubey's company in a crowded, confused scene. At the same time, Brigadier General R.O. Tyler was sent to Belle Plain to organize the chaos that had developed at that point. He was directed to gather well men into brigades to be forwarded to the front as quickly as possible.

On May 16, the 400 men of the 15th started to work early in the morning repairing the roads some three miles beyond Belle Plain. According to Benham, the roads "...will probably be put in very good order, as to all the worst places, in the course of two or three days, which my own reconnaissance confirms, although, perhaps, while they are being much used, it may be expedient to continue a company or part of a company in the care of them, or some pioneer workers from the infantry here, if the engineers are needed elsewhere." Part of the depot company of the 15th was put to work on the pontoon wharves.[16]

On May 17, as lines of supply trains developed to cross the one bridge south at Fredericksburg, in what became yet another major bottleneck, Benham received orders to get another bridge built at that point. He was also told to bring the 15th back to Washington once the work around Belle Plain was done. Colonel William H. Pettes, of the 50th New York, back at the Engineer Depot in Washington, was ordered at noon on the seventeenth to fit out, and be ready to send, a train of 24 pontoons on to Belle Plain. Several hours later Pettes was further directed to fit out a train of forty boats and material for Harper's Ferry.

Pettes received movement orders and sent the train to Belle Plain by 10 a.m. on the eighteenth, and later that afternoon, the train to Harper's Ferry under guard of a detachment from the 1st District of Columbia Volunteer Infantry.[17]

On May 17 the 50th arrived at the army's headquarters near the Spotsylvania Court House. The next morning the regiment broke camp, moving two miles to the right, except for Company I, which was left behind until noon to build a corduroy road before rejoining the regiment.[18]

On May 21 Benham reported from Belle Plain to the army's chief of staff, Major General A.A. Humphreys:

> The roads are now essentially in very good condition between this and Fredericksburg, and I expect to withdraw the command from them tomorrow, except one large company for the care of the bridges and the repairs of the roads. The bridge received from Washington on the 19th for that place was sent over as early as it was possible to procure transportation from the quartermaster's department, the last half of the animals only being supplied at 4 a.m. to-day. I ordered the bridge to be laid (to replace the pontoons from the front) this fore-noon, and I doubt not that it was so laid.
>
> In the anticipation that possibly all animals may be otherwise needed, I have also directed the officer there in case that his bridges move by water, to raft them with the trucks on the rafts ready for towing, and to comply with calls of the military governor of Fredericksburg, or other superior officer there. The large amount of bridge material here will be got ready for moving as far as circumstances will permit.[19]

On May 23, Benham was ordered to place a pontoon bridge at Port Royal for Abercrombie's brigade to use in its march south.[20] "We had orders to be ready to start at a moments notice," wrote Deloss Burton of the 50th New York Engineers home on May 22 at nine in the morning, "but did not however until 1 PM yesterday being among the last to leave. Within half an hour after we left the Rebs had the ground. We expected to have bridged the Mattapony [sic] river here, and should have but our cavalry came upon the enemy's pickets so suddenly, they had not time to destroy the bridge, which saves us the trouble of building a pontoon. The Rebs were making preparations for a strong stand here. Had already finished about half a mile of very good earthworks."[21] The next morning Burton's compatriots marched off, reaching the North Anna around two in the afternoon.

Men of the 50th completed building a bridge across the North Anna at Jericho Mill between 4 and 4:30 p.m. on the twenty-third. As soon as the last bulk was secured, the V Corps artillery chief, Charles Wainwright, ordered six batteries—24 12-pounder cannon, each weighing two tons—to cross, which they did successfully. Brigadier General Lysander Cutler's division followed, putting three quarters of the V Corps across in a successful beachhead.[22]

"At a brick church about 1 mile from the North Side the army separated, the 2d corps taking the main road leading to Richmond and the 5th Corps a road to the right, the 6th Corps remaining behind as a reserve," Burton wrote on the twenty-fourth. "Our train going with the 5th and Company I with the 2nd. When we reached the river about 1 division of the 5th Corps were across the river, it being fordable in low water. As soon as we arrived here commenced our bridge & finished it in an hour & a half. The infantry were the first to cross, then the artillery."[23]

Company I of the 50th built two bridges across the North Anna River to replace a railroad bridge Confederate infantry had fired before retreating on May 24. The next day they built a third bridge in that area. But on the twenty-sixth other engineers having put together more permanent wooden bridges, Company I took up their temporary pontoon bridges and headed towards Chesterfield and Federal cavalry.

Benham was then ordered, on May 26, to move from the Engineer Depot in Washington to Fortress Monroe with all the bridging material available and there to be ready to move up the James River at short notice.[24] He left behind Pettes and a number of men from the 50th New York to continue building more bridging material, such as pontoons and barges.

Special Orders No. 56 Washington D.C. May 26th. 1864

I. - Private James Lennon 15th Regt N.Y.V.E. on duty in the Quarter Masters Department, is hereby returned to his regiment.

I.I. Peter Flynn Co "C" 15th N.Y.V.E. is hereby detailed for duty in the Qr Mrs Dept of this command, until further orders, and will report immediately to Capt Hull A.Q.M.

Captain Slosson found his equipment short 400 chesses, 500 balk lashings, two coil cables, and 25 long balks of building the needed bridge at Port Royal and requested this equipment from Benham on May 28.[25] Material was sent on, and the 460-foot-long bridge was completed by June 5.[26] Slosson then went on to Fort Monroe to meet up with the rest of the brigade then in Virginia, arriving there the sixth.

"Have writen [sic] a long letter giving your some idea of what were doing up to the 26th," Burton wrote home May 30, "were then at a place called Jeric[h]o Mills on the North Anna. The morning of the 26th took up our bridge & came here [Dabney's Ferry], the distance of about 40 miles &

built another bridge in a bout 24 hours. This is the Pamunky River about 12 miles above White House Landing & 17 from Richmond."

The bridge building was anything but smooth, Burton reported:

About 500 yards from the ferry the cavalry halted and sent down a few skirmishers who concealed themselves among the trees and bushes each side of the road and commenced firing. We then came up with our train & put together a couple of boats which we took on shoulders and carried to within about 100 yards of the river. As the road runs paralel [sic] with the river we could not be seen till within 20 yards of the bank. The 1st Michigan then came up and formed in front of us. When all were ready Brig. General [George A.] Custer gave the order to forward with a whoop & a yell. The 1st Michigan were armed with the Spencer carbine (seven shooter) and such shooting & yelling ought to have frightind [sic] a whole regiment of Rebs, but did not till they saw our cannon boats coming on the double quick, which they took for some infernal machines & took to their heels. We launched our boats which were loaded in less than a minute & taken across as quickly as possible. Then commenced our bridge and had it ready in about an hour & the cavalry began to cross."[27]

General Orders No. 21 Washington May 27th 1864

The ponton and infantry drills of the portion of the Brigade now here will be resumed at once according to former instructions - the arrangements being made as far as practicable for all the troops not employed in the Workshifts or otherwise indispensably absent to drill at ponton drill, both with canvas and wooden pontons at the usual hours every morning and at Infantry drills every afternoon except saturday.

The drills of the 15th Regiment to be by battalion every Monday, Wednesday and Friday afternoons

Hereafter when the troops of either of the regiments of the brigade require pontons and bridge material for drill, the senior officer present of such regiment will make a requisition on the officer in charge of the property at the depot for such boats and bridge material as he may required, duly receipting for the same, and he will be responsible to these Head Quarters for the due care and preservation of the same after every drill and when he shall leave the Depot, or when this property shall be required for other purposes - he will also be required to enquire into, and account for, immediately in relation to any loss or destruction of such property which may occur. To this end he is directed to have an inspection of the same by some officer of his regiment - at the close of each drill - so that he may at once be apprised of and enabled to act upon any neglect of duty of his subordinates in regard to such property.

Certainly the engineers in the field had neither the time nor the inclination to do pontoon laying drills at the end of May. Company I laid yet another bridge on the evening of the twenty-seventh to allow Federal cavalry to chase Confederate skirmishers near Hanovertown. At midnight they took up the bridges and started to Huntley's Crossing, several miles upriver. They reached that spot near daybreak, and the weary engineers went to work laying their pontoon bridge down yet again. Major General George G. Meade, commander of the Army of the Potomac, himself crossed on this bridge, which the company was able to leave in place until May 30. At that time they took up the bridge again, and returned to Huntley's Crossing to get some well-earned rest. "The company, considering the hard work they have done, is in good condition, and we all feel as though we would sacrifice anything if it will only put down the rebellion," Lieutenant Owen reported.[28]

Special Orders No. 57 Washington D.C. May 28th 1864

I. Private Patrick Larkin Co "B" & Private Edward Burke Co "C" 15th N.Y.V. Engineers, are hereby detailed for duty in the Qr. Mrs. Dept. of this Brigade, and will report as soon as possible to Capt Alex Hull A.Q.M.

I.I. Private Peter Flynn of Co. "C" 15th N.Y.V. Engrs, on duty at these Head Quarters, in the Qr. Mrs. Dept; is hereby returned to his regiment for duty.

Benham himself arrived at Fort Monroe, with the rest of his brigade, save those working on equipment back in Washington, on two small steamers, on May 31 and reported there for orders from Grant or Meade.[29] He and his men managed to scrape together 1,460 yards of pontoon bridging and a siege train complete with all necessary tools. Late in the evening orders arrived from Halleck that he was to forward all the pontoons to Major General Benjamin Butler's Army of the James.[30] Benham then forwarded all the bridging material he had on hand to Butler's army, while himself remaining at Fortress Monroe.

64

The volunteer engineers not only built these facilities at City Point, Virginia, through which the Army of the Potomac was supplied during the siege of Petersburg, they also made up the post's defending garrison.

Library of Congress

These infantrymen and cannoneers practice crossing a waterway on a pontoon. They would cross under fire to protect engineers building bridges.

Library of Congress

A pontoon bridge laid by volunteer engineers across the James River.

Library of Congress

The interior of Fort Sedgwick, part of the line outside Petersburg, shows, near left, the wicker baskets called gabions that the engineers made.

Library of Congress

68

The brass enlisted cap badge of the Corps of Engineers.

Author's collection

A first lieutenant of engineers; the light blue trousers suggest that he is a volunteer rather than a regular officer who would have more likely worn dark blue trousers with yellow piping down each leg. He holds a foot officer's sword and wears the regulation Corps of Engineers cap badge of a silver castle within a gold wreath.

The chapel built by men of the Volunteer Engineer Brigade in their camp outside of Petersburg during the winter of 1864-65. The skills of the brigade's officers and men led to its camp always being the best in the entire army in terms of comfort and appearance.

Officers of the 15th New York Volunteer Engineer Regiment at their regimental headquarters. They are as they would be dressed for the field, in comfortable slouch hats (the field-grade officer in the center wears only a castle without a wreath for a cap badge). Behind them are their regimental colors, the dark blue regimental color bearing the coat of arms of the state of New York. The engineer private on the left stands guard with infantry accouterments.

National Archives

Colonel Barton S. Alexander begun the training of the New York Volunteer Engineer regiments in Washington. He wears his uniform as he would in the field, with a nonregulation cloak and tall white gaiters designed to keep his trousers clean.

Library of Congress

These wagons carry the heavy wooden pontoon boats used for bridges designed to bear a great deal of traffic. Similar canvas boats built around a wooden frame were used for short-term river crossings where time was more important than durability.

Author's collection

74

Volunteer engineers laid these pontoon bridges across the James River at Richmond after that city was abandoned by the Confederates and the bridges were burned by their retreating forces in April 1865.
Author's collection

These privates of Company B, U.S. Engineer Battalion, wear the standard fatigue dress of enlisted engineers in the field, a four-button dark blue blouse, plain sky blue trousers, and a variety of issue forage caps and slouch hats with the castle insignia of the Corps of Engineers displayed on their fronts.

Library of Congress

The Wilderness, May 10, 1864.

Engineers using axes "slash" a front in the Federal lines during the Battle of the Wilderness. They first erected a line of wooden works, then began clearing away trees, leaving stumps to make attacking across the ground more difficult.

Frank Leslie's Illustrated Weekly

Their knapsacks piled on the left front, engineers begin building breastworks in the Wilderness campaign.

Edwin Forbes

78

Edwin Forbes

These engineers build a pontoon bridge while under enemy fire.

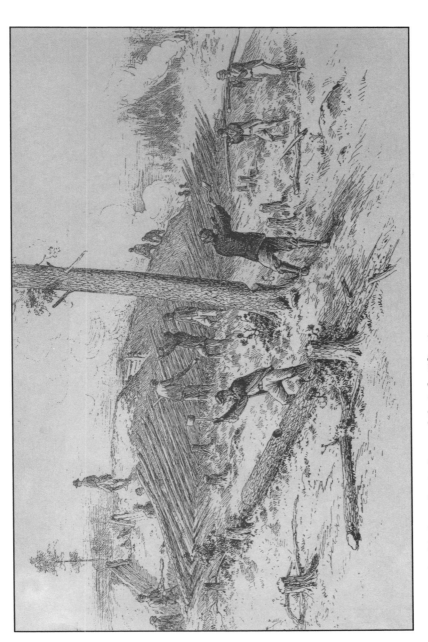

Engineers build obstacles in front of their fortifications.

Edwin Forbes

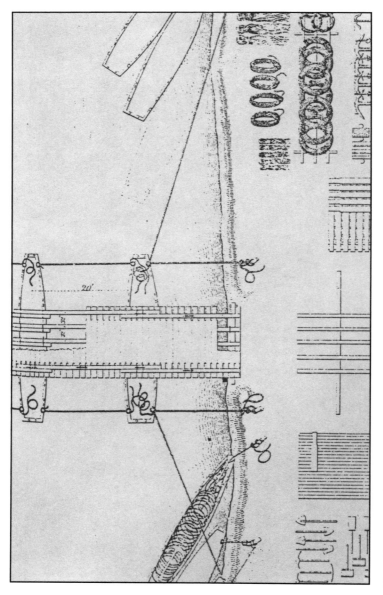

This illustration from Duane's manual for the engineers shows how a pontoon bridge is constructed.

81

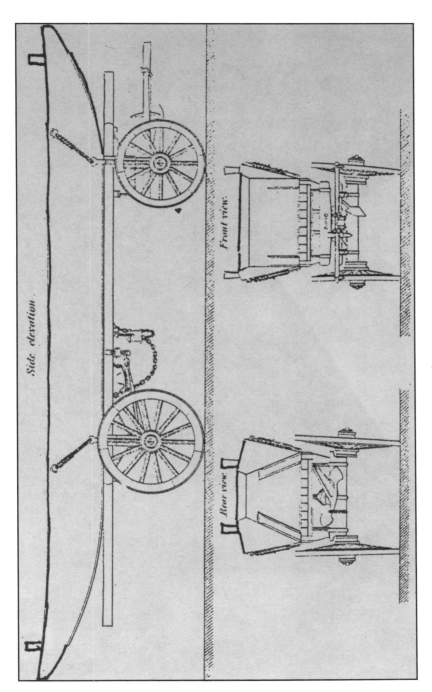

The French pontoon and carriage from Duane's manual.

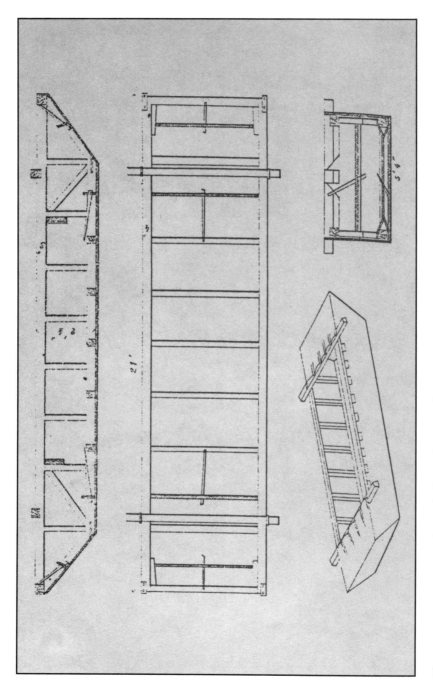

The canvas pontoon as shown in Duane's manual.

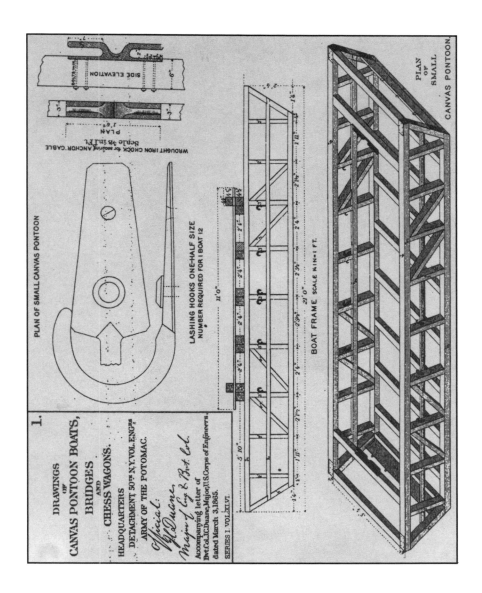

PLAN OF SMALL CANVAS PONTOON

SIDE ELEVATION

PLAN

WROUGHT IRON CHOCK for securing ANCHOR CABLE
Scale ½ in. I Ft.

LASHING HOOKS ONE-HALF SIZE
NUMBER REQUIRED FOR I BOAT 12

1.

DRAWINGS
OF
CANVAS PONTOON BOATS,
BRIDGES
AND
CHESS WAGONS.

HEADQUARTERS
DETACHMENT 50TH N.Y. VOL. ENGRS
ARMY OF THE POTOMAC.

Official:
J.C. Duane
Major of Eng & Bvt. Col.

Accompanying letter of
Bvt Col., J.C Duane, Major, U.S Corps of Engineers.
dated March 3, 1865.

SERIES 1 VOL.XLVI.

BOAT FRAME SCALE ¼ IN = 1 FT.

PLAN
OF
SMALL
CANVAS PONTOON.

84

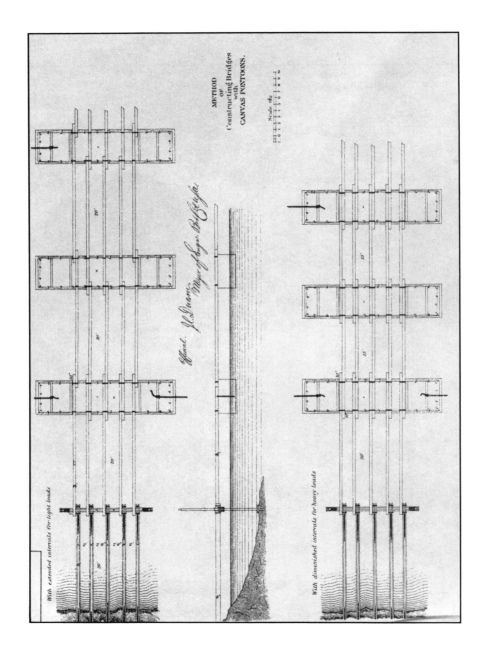

METHOD
OF
Constructing Bridges
with
CANVAS PONTOONS.

Scale 1/64

With extended intervals for light loads

With diminished intervals for heavy loads

85

Building breastworks on the Cold Harbor line. Note the wooden barricades built as a retaining wall against which the dirt from the ditch in front was thrown. The men have fixed their bayonets and stuck their rifled muskets into the ground— a reminder that engineers may be called on to fight as infantry at any moment.

Battles & Leaders of the Civil War

This picket post in front of Fort Sedgwick, in the Petersburg lines, was made by placing gabions around in a semi-circle, then laying more gabions on their tops.

Battles & Leaders of the Civil War

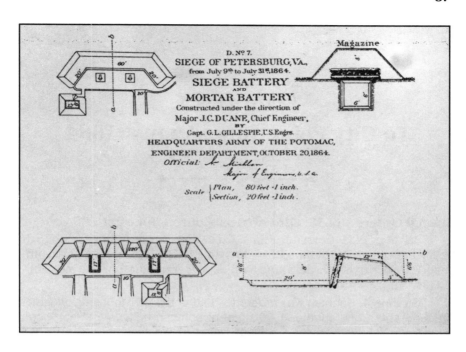

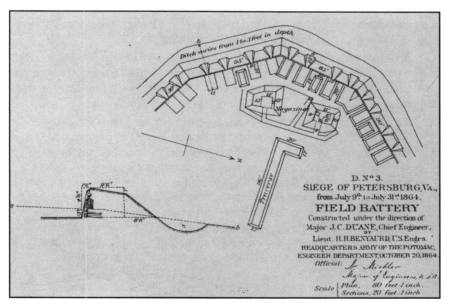

Siege of Petersburg, Virginia

Plans for siege battery and mortar battery as well as field battery.

Atlas to Accompany the Official Records of the Union and Confederate Armies 1861–1865

CHAPTER 5
To City Point: June–August 1864

◀──────────▶

Special Orders No. 58, Off Fortress Monroe, June 1st 1864

Privates W.H. Garrison, Chas. Cole, and Abram Came Co E, 15th
N.Y.V.E. are hereby detailed for duty in the Qr. M. Dept. of this com-
mand until further orders and will report immediately to Capt Hull
A.Q.M.

On June 4, Benham was ordered to gather the 400-foot-long bridge at
Fredericksburg and another 1,200 feet of pontoon bridges that had been
sent from New York to the Engineer Depot in Washington since he had
arrived at Fortress Monroe. The New York bridge equipment included 33
pontoons, 100 chesses, 6 trestles, 420 common balks, 170 claw balks,
and other necessary material.[1] He also sent on Slosson's company to Bermuda Hundred to build bridges for Butler's troops.

A detachment of some 50 men of Company I, 50th New York, was
ordered to accompany the cavalry with a pontoon train of eight boats on
their drive around the Confederate left. "The 6th, we crossed the river
Pamunkey at New Castle," Owen wrote home June 20.

> We then proceeded northwest and on the 11th met the enemy near
> Trevilian Station, 9 miles east of Gordonsville. Fought all day and drive
> the enemy out. The 12th, moved up to the Station, fought all day, drove
> the enemy the first part of the day, but suffered a heavy loss. Took
> several hundred prisoners. On the night of the 12th, fell back very fast,
> having expended nearly all the ammunition, and the enemy having to[o]
> strong a force for us to withstand. We then came back passing through
> Spotsylvania Court House, Bowling Green, thence to King and Queen
> Court House where we lay on the night of the 18th. Yesterday, we came
> back to this place where we are now crossing the Mattaponi on the way,
> I expect, to White House.[2]

While bridging went on, other engineers began entrenching, building
field works. Burton of the 50th New York wrote home on June 7: "Our men

88

are building some large forts which when completed will start them (the Rebs) out of here in a hurry." Still, this was not a major part of engineer work to date. "We expected to have to take a hand in the sieging operations but think our company will be the last called upon & none of the engineers have called upon yet. The work so far has been done by the infantry who now take hold of the spade & pick with a will," Burton wrote home.[3]

Butler requested Benham to join his headquarters on June 9, but Benham declined, explaining that "The orders of General Meade are so distinct for me to remain herewith my special material until his further orders, or those of General Grant, should the presence of myself, men, and material be necessary with you, would not this be safely accomplished for me by an order of Colonel Comstock, now with you, given in the name of General Grant?"[4]

By June 10 Butler had no further need of pontoon bridges, and Captain James L. Robbins of the brigade, who had been assigned to build and repair them, was ordered to return to Fortress Monroe and report to Benham.[5]

Special Orders No. 59 Fortress Monroe June 10th. 1864

I. Private Frederick Hamilton Co A and James Cornelison Co H 50th N.Y.V.E. are hereby detailed for duty in the Brigade Band until further orders, and will report to these Hd. Qrs. as soon as possible.

I.I. - Lieut G.W. Nares A.C.S. is hereby authorized to proceed to Washington on important Commissary Business. Having completed which he will return to this post on [or] before the 16th inst.

Lieut Nares will, on his return take charge of all convalescents and other men who may be at the Engineer Depot, belonging to this command, and who are ready to rejoin their companies.

By June 12, Benham was able to report that his equipment at the fortress included 155 wooden pontoons, enough for 3,100 feet. He was short of chesses, but ordered the troops back in Washington to make more and forward it as quickly as possible.[6]

On June 13 all the bridge material, amounting to some 3,100 feet worth, was sent to Fort Powhatan on the James River, and Benham arrived there on the afternoon of the fifteenth. There he arrived just in time to oversee the completion of a bridge across the James that used some 104 boats to cover 2,200 feet, volunteer engineers working from the west end, and engineers of the Regular Army on the east end. The army would take three days to cross this bridge.[7]

June 12 also found Lieutenant Colonel Ira Spaulding's detachment of the 50th camped near Cold Harbor, where troops under Major Brainerd were repairing roads near Bottom's Bridge to be ready for the arrival of II Corps. That evening one of his pontoon trains, under Major Ford, bridged the Chickahominy under fire of Confederates. One man of Company K was mortally wounded while working on the bridge.

On June 14 Brainerd's battalion was ordered to the James River where two companies spent the day repairing wharves for use of the II Corps, then crossing in transports. Beers' battalion spent the day building permanent bridges over each branch of the Chickahominy at Jones', near his pontoon bridges. After these jobs were finished, two battalions again joined under Spaulding at the Chickahominy where they laid a bridge some 1,240 feet long with timber and corduroy approaches of some 450 more feet.

The fifteenth was spent in moving to new positions, Brainerd's battalion reaching just outside Petersburg the next day. As Grant pressed on, the post at White Horse, Port Royal, was abandoned by June 16, and the bridging material there was ordered returned to Washington.[8]

On June 16 Benham ordered his headquarters to come to his camp at Fort Powhatan or, if he had already moved on by the time they arrived, to City Point. The headquarters was to include the brigade staff, and guard with one wagon, a horse for each officer, and four extra horses for orderlies. They were to bring rations enough to last for five days. An assistant surgeon was to stay behind to care for the men unable to make the march to Benham's new headquarters.

On the seventeenth Major Ford, who, "for some weeks had been too ill to walk or sit on his horse and had received a leave of absence for twenty days, when at Long Bridge on the Chickahominy, but he did not feel disposed to leave his command until it arrived at the James River, when he turned over the command of his battalion to Captain McDonald and left for the North."[9]

The bridge at Fort Powhatan was taken up by 3 a.m. on June 18 and then was brought to City Point by water, the men using the pontoons as boats. There they landed and went into camp on the banks of the Appomattox. The men began repairing the worn bridging equipment. Captain Lubey took a detachment with 36 boats to Jones' Landing to build a new bridge there, something his men completed on June 21. Another detachment of the 15th was sent to build a road from the landing at City Point to the quartermaster's corrals, where the army's mounts were housed. This task was finished by the 27th.

In the meantime, on the eighteenth, Spaulding divided the extra train of boats among his three battalions. The result was that the first battalion had 15 boats; the second, 15 boats; and the third, 14 boats. All the trains moved that day to a point near Old Church, about two miles from City Point where eventually they would all spend most of the war. Between then and July 29, "all the available officers and men of this command not required for repairing and guarding the trains were occupied in front of Petersburg, making gabions and fascines, working upon forts, covered ways, roads, and bridges, about 1,200 fascines and 10,000 gabions have during that time been made by the men of this command," Spaulding reported.[10] The emphasis had changed from bridging to fortification building.

"From the moment the Federal troops appeared before Petersburg," a Union officer of engineers later wrote, "the duties of the Engineer Corps were very exacting. Every man was engaged in superintending and assisting in the construction of the technical part of the siege-works."[11]

An officer in the opposing force's Corps of Engineers, Lieutenant Colonel W.W. Blackford, 1st Regiment of Engineer Troops, reported the activities of his troops were virtually identical to those in the Volunteer Engineer Brigade:

> The main body of the regiment was engaged in manufacturing siege material, particularly chevaux-de-frise to be placed just over the crest of the parapet of the trench. These chevaux-de-frise were pine logs ten or twelve feet long and eight or ten inches in diameter, along which at spaces of about a foot, holes were bored through at right angles. Through these holes strong poles were driven projecting three feet on each side and sharpened at the ends. The logs were fastened together end to end with chains and then rolled down the slope in front of the parapet to arrest a sudden dash of the enemy, and they made an exceedingly awkward thing to cross, with a line of muskets firing from the crest of the bank.[12]

Company C, 50th New York left City Point with 36 pontoon boats on June 20, abound for Butler's Army of the James at Bermuda Hundred. They reached there that evening, after freeing one that had run aground as they were being towed down river. They were finally unloaded and moved down the river bank to Jones' Neck opposite Federal infantry where, at one in the morning, the men began laying down a bridge. It was completed by late afternoon the following day and consisted of 27 pontoon boats and 29 bays.

Company I, 50th New York took to the road again, leaving White House on the late hours of June 22, the same day that the 1st Battalion went into the line as infantry in front of the Jones house, near Petersburg. On the evening of the twenty-third they reached Wilson's Landing, leaving there on the twenty-fourth and arriving at Debson's Landing with the Cavalry Corps on the morning of the twenty-fifth. There, according to Owen, they "have been very busy helping cross the Cavalry Corps ever since. We brought with us from White House an immense wagon train, about 800 wagons in all. These all have to be ferried over in steamers and as the landing is not very good, it is slow work. The train will all be over today. We have not taken the pontons over yet as we have part of our bridge in use for a dock way."[13]

General Order No. 22 City Point Va June 29th 1864

I Commanding Officers of Regiments and Detachments of this Brigade, will muster their men for pay on the 30th inst.

I.I: The Infantry and Ponton drills of this command will be resumed at once & be continued whenever practicable.

Gen Orders No. 19 of May 9th from these Head Quarters are modified as follows.

           Drill 8 1/2 to 9 1/2 A.M.   Dress Parade 6 1/2 P.M.
           Do 4 to 6 P.M.   Supper 7 "

It was hard keeping up with paying the men when the army was on the move. Lieutenant Owen wrote home June 28, "I cannot tell when I will get [paid]. I have a little money with me and will send you some."[14] According to Army Regulations, "Troops will be mustered for pay on the last day of February, April, June, August, October, and December."[15]

Special Orders No. 60 City Point Va. June 25th. 1864

Capt Stephen Chester Commissary of Musters of this command is hereby directed to proceed to Washington D.C. on business connected with his Department, there to await further orders.

Special Orders No. 61 City Point, June 26th. 1864

I - During the temporary absence of Capt S. Chester, Lieut F.S. Livingston A.D.C. will act as Brigade Inspector.

I.I. - Private Wm. Jackson Co B, 15th N.Y.V.E. is hereby detailed for duty as Blacksmith, in the Qr. Masters Dept of this command till further orders, to date from May 18th. 1864.

On July 1 a train of 20 canvas boats complete with necessary equipment arrived at the City Point camp from Washington. The next day, Benham assigned a detachment from the 15th to work with the engineers already building defensive works at City Point, a job that lasted throughout the month of July.

Company I, 50th New York, with the Cavalry Corps, crossed the James River on steamers, landing at Windmill Point the morning of the twenty-ninth. That afternoon they headed to City Point, arriving there on the morning of the thirtieth, then going into camp with the rest of the engineers.

Special Orders No. 62 City Point Va, July 4th. 1864

A General Court Martial is hereby appointed to meet at the quarters of Lieut Roosa Ambulance Corps on the 5th day of July 1864, or as soon thereafter as practicable for the trial of Private F. Halloran Co A 50th N.Y.V.E. and such other prisoners as may be brought before it.

Detail for the Court.

1	Major W.A. Ketchum 15th N.Y.V.E.		4 Lieut K.S. O'Keeffe 15th N.Y.V.E.
2	Capt H.V. Slosson	Do	5 Lieut R.O.S. Burke Do
3	Capt J.L. Robbins 50th	Do	

Lieut F.S. Livingston A.D.C. Judge Advocate

No other officers than those named can be assembled without manifest injury to the Service.

A national holiday, most engineers celebrated the Fourth of July in a more festive manner than writing special orders. "On the 4th I went up to the front," Lieutenant Owen wrote home, "where I participated in a fine Fourth of July dinner given by the 1st Battalion, 50th New York Volunteer Engineers, commanded by Major Brainerd. It was a fine affair and did honor to its *donors*."[16]

Special Orders No. 63 City Point Va July 8th 1864

The cases of Privates Cusick & Dwyer alias Daily, Bailey, alias a citizen, in the opinion of the General Commanding requiring immediate example the Genl. Court Martial now in session at these Head Quarters, is hereby directed to extend its sessions on the 8th & 9th. days of July 1864, until the hours of 7 P.M.

On July 10 Spaulding sent orders for a train of 18 canvas pontoon boats to join the Cavalry Corps. They would stay with the cavalry until Major General Philip Sheridan would be recalled to command in the Valley of Virginia, that August, when the train would return to City Point. On the same day all battalions of the 50th were consolidated under Spaulding's command to work on the lines at Petersburg.

General Order No. 23 City Point Va. July 11th 1864

I. Before a General Court Martial of which Major W.A. Ketchum 15th N.Y.V. Engineers is President, convened at Head Qrs. Engineer Brigade A-o-P by virtue of Special Orders 11st 62. from Head Quarters Engineer Brigade of July 4th 1864 were arraigned and tried.

1 Private Francis M. Halloran Co "A" 50th N.Y.V. Engrs upon the following

Charge - Conduct prejudicial to good order and military discipline
Finding - Guilty
Sentence - To forfeit his monthly pay for three (3) calendar months.

2 Private Patrick Cusick Co B 15th N.Y.V.E. upon the following
Charge - Offering violence to his superior officer
Finding - Not Guilty
and the Court does therefore acquit him.

I.I.: The proceedings Findings and Sentences in the above cases having been submitted to the General Commanding Brigade, the following are the orders thereon.

The Sentence of Private Francis M. Halloran Co "A" 50th N.Y.V.E. is approved, and his commanding Officer will see that it is executed.

The Proceedings & Finding in the case of Private Patrick Cusick Co B 15th N.Y.V.E. are approved and he will be returned to duty.

On July 12 Company I, 50th New York, was assigned permanently to the Cavalry Corps and joined that organization's headquarters at Light House Point on the James. The company brought with it 42 wagons, with some 252 mules and 18 canvas pontoon boats. The company was capable of bridging some 400 feet of water.

Special Orders No. 64 City Point Va July 28th/64

Lieut A.H. Mogany 15th N.Y.V.E. is hereby detailed as Act Asst Qr. Master of this command and will take charge of all property belonging to this command now at Fortress Monroe Va.

The above date is printed as written, but, judging from the dates on later orders, is dated incorrectly. The headquarters clerks were still in a state of some confusion. The order probably dates from the eighth.

General Order No. 24 City Point Va. July 18th 1864

Hereafter except otherwise specially ordered, the drills of this command will be as follows.

A ponton drill from 8 1/2 A.M. each morning - Sundays excepted - to continue two hours or until the designated practice is completed. A Company drill on Monday, Wednesday and Friday afternoons, for about two hours from 4 P.M. and a Battalion drill on Tuesday and Thursday afternoon at the same hours. Dress Parade will be had each day at 6 1/2 P.M.

At all such drills and parades all officers of the command will be present acting and directing according to their respective ranks or grades unless specially excused in writing by the Surgeon - or from these Head Quarters or unavoidably detained by other duties, - excepting only the actual officer of the Guard - the officer of the Guard for Ponton drill, and the field officers from company drills - for which his general supervision it is expected will be sufficient.

It was obvious that long hours and dirty work in the field were over now that the army was sitting in what appeared to be permanent works around Petersburg. Dress parades, in which each man was to show up in his dress frock coat with his brass brightly polished and his boots neatly blackened, were not things seen while on campaign.

Special Orders No. 65 City Point Va July 18th. 1864

The General Court Martial convened by Special Orders No. 62 of July 4th/64 from these Head Quarters and of which Major W.A. Ketchum 15th N.Y.V.E. is President, is hereby dissolved.

Special Orders No. 66 City Point Va. July 16th 1864

Surg. I.Z. Gibbs 15th N.Y.V. Engineers is hereby directed to proceed with eleven (11) sick men to Washington where he will place them under the charge of the Surgeon in charge of the Hospital at the engineer Depot.

Having completed his business, Surgeon Gibbs will return immediately to these Head Quarters.

On July 21 Benham sent another 30 boats with necessary equipment to Captain Lubey at Jones' Neck.

Special Orders No. 67 City Point Va July 24th 1864

Corpl. A.I. Brown, Co "A" 15th N.Y.V. Engineers, is hereby detailed as Brigade Mail Carrier, and will report to these Head Quarters immediately.

Army regulations did not allow a post of "brigade mail carrier" in a headquarters. Yet, especially in an army made up of nonprofessional soldiers, mail to and from home was about the most important morale booster there was. "Letters are the only links a soldier has to bind him to civilization," one major wrote home, "and no one but a soldier knows how highly he prizes them."[17]

A mail carrier was, therefore, considered one of the most important men in the brigade by his fellow soldiers. "I know of no reason why we should not get our mail from home regularly as other regiments do," one irate volunteer engineer officer, who had missed his mail for some time, wrote home May 20.[18]

On July 26 Captain Slosson and his men laid a bridge some 36 boats long at Broadway Landing on the Appomattox.

Special Orders No. 68 City Point Va July 29th 1864.

I - Capt I.L. Robbins with two men will proceed to Washington and will take command of that portion of his company ("A") which is not stationed at the Workshops at the Engineer Depot.

I.I. Lieut E.C. Byram Co "A" 50th N.Y.V. Engineers on being relieved by Capt. Robbins at the Engineer Depot Washington D.C. will immediately join that portion of his company which is now stationed at this place.

On July 29 Benham sent Lieutenant O'Keefe with a train of some 36 boats to Deep Bottom, understanding they were needed there. It turned out to be a false alarm, and the train returned to City Point the next day.

Special Orders No. 69 City Point Va. Aug 1st. 1864

The following named privates are hereby detailed for duty in the Qr. Mrs. Dept. of this command until further orders, and will report immediately to Lieut Templeton A.Q.M.

Michael J. Halloran	Co "A" 50th N.Y.V. Engineers
James Coles	" B 15th " " " "
James Hayes	" A " " " " "

General Order No. 25 City Point Va. Aug 2nd 1864

Special Orders No. 64 of June 28th 1864 from these Head Qrs appointing Lieut A.H. Megary 15th N.Y.V. Engineers act. asst. Q.M. is hereby revoked and Lieut Megary will until further orders act as commissary of Subsistence for this command.

Special Orders No 70 City Point, Aug 3rd. 1864

Corpl John Jones Co. "A" 15th N.Y.V.E. is hereby detailed for duty in the Commissary Dept. of this command until further orders and will report immediately to Lieut A.H. Megary A.C.S.

Special Orders No. 71 City Point Va. Aug 7th 1864

Special Orders No. 70 of Aug 3rd/64 from these Head Qrs. are hereby revoked, and Corpl John Jones Co. "A" 15th N.Y.V.E. is returned to his regiment for duty.

General Order No. 26 City Point VA Aug 11th 1864

I. Capt J.T. Elliott C.S. having been assigned to duty as commissary of Subsistence of this Brigade by Special Orders 10 & 210 Hd Qrs A-o-P. will as early as practicable relieve Lieut A.H. Megany A.A.c.S. of the duties.

I.I: As soon as relieved from such duties, and the proper transfer papers and reports shall have been made, Lieut. Megany will report to Major Ketchum, for duty with his regiment.

In thus relieving Lieut. Megany of these commissary duties by an officer of that Staff Corps. as directed from General Head Qrs. the Commanding General desires to express his satisfaction with the faithful and efficient manner in which Lieut Megany has performed these and other staff duties, with which he has been entrusted, during this past one or two months.

Bringing in a full-time staff officer from the outside allowed the regiment to return a trained engineer, then doing work as a commissary officer, back to where he would be most useful, with his line company.

Special Orders No. 72 City Point Va. Aug 11th. 1864

In compliance with summons of a Court Martial Lieuts W.R. Marsh and K.S.O'Keefe wil proceed to Washington D.C. reporting immediately on arrival to Col W.H. Pettes comd'g Engineer Depot, they will return at once to this place as soon as they finish their testimony before the court.

Special Orders No. 73 City Point Va. Aug 15th. 1864.

I. Private James Hayes Co "A" 15th N.Y.V. E. on duty at these Headquarters, is hereby returned to his Regiment.

I.I. Private William Wicks Co. "A" 15th N.Y.V.E. is hereby detailed for duty in the Quarter Masters Department of this command and he will report immediately to Lt. Templeton A.Q.M.

By August 20 the works around Petersburg were so near completion that engineers were sent to prepare the way for works west of the line, on the extreme Union left flank.

Special Orders No. 74 City Point Va. Aug 21st 1864.

Sergeant David M. Campbell Co. "C" 15th N.Y.V.E. is hereby detailed for duty in the Commissary Dept of the Brigade, and will report to Capt. Elliott - C.S.

Special Orders No. 75 City Point Va. Aug 22nd. 1864

Lieut P.C. Kingsland A.D.C. will proceed to Washington in charge of two barges loaded with Engineer Property, which he will turn over to Col W.H. Pettes Comd'g Engr Depot, Washington.

Having accomplished his business Lieut Kingsland will return immediately to these Head Qrs.

On August 26 troops from the 50th were sent to build redoubts to the left of the line on the Weldon Railroad, Burn Chimney, and the Strong house.

General Order No. 27 City Point Va. Aug 28th 1864

Commanding Officers of Regiments and Detachments in this Brigade will muster their men for pay on the 31st inst.

Special Orders No. 76, City Point Va, Aug 31st. 1864

1st Lieut Geo Templeton A.Q.M. of this command is hereby directed to proceed to Washington D.C. with servant, on important public business and return to this camp on Sept 3rd. 1864.

Officers were authorized to bring servants, who would be doing such tasks as their cooking and cleaning, with them into the field. Many employed escaped slaves who developed close bonds with their employers. According to regulations, servants were not to wear any part of the regulation army uniform but had to carry "with him a certificate from the officer who employs him, verified, for regimental officers, by the signature of the Colonel. For other officers under the rank of Colonel, by the chief of their corps or department."[19]

CHAPTER 6
At City Point:
September–December 1864
▶──────────◀

General Order No. 28 City Point Va. Sept 1st 1864

General Order No. 22 & 24 of June 29th & July 18 1864 from these Head Quarters, are hereby modified as follows.

Dress Parade 5 1/2 P.M. - Instead of	6 1/2 P.M
Supper 6 " " " "	7 "

Special Orders No. 77, City Point Va. Sept 5th. 1864

I. Capt J.T. Elliott having been assigned to this command as Commissary of Subsistance, Lieut. Geo W. Wares A.C.S. is hereby relieved from his duties.

I.I. Lieut Geo W. Wares with Servant, Corpls Chas Angus and Brainerd of the Commissary Department, will proceed to Washington and remain until the Detachment of mustered out men belonging to their regiment, 50th N.Y. Engrs. arrives, when they will join them and proceed to Elmira N.Y.

Men who had joined the original regiment in 1861 had begun to reach the end of their three-year enlistments and were now being allowed to muster out. Many were replaced with poorly motivated draftees and paid substitutes so that, in many ways, the quality of the Army of the Potomac fell off by late 1864.

Special Orders No. 78, City Point Va, Sept 5th 1864

Surgeon Chas N. Hewitt 50th N.Y.V.E. Surgeon in chief of this command, will proceed to the Engineer Depot Washington D.C. for the purpose of inspecting the condition of the sick now there in the Brigade Hospital. Having completed this inspection, Surgeon Hewitt will return to his duties at this place.

By September 7 the redoubts being built on the Union left were so well along that they were able to get to work on the finishing touches, the wire entanglements, abatis, fraises, and slashing in the brush. "Many miles of corduroy roads and bridges had been built by the Fiftieth New York Volunteer Engineers," the army's chief engineer reported, "for the convenience of and more direct communication between the different corps of the army."

Special Orders No. 79 City Point Va, Sept 7th. 1864

Private James McDonald Co B 15th. N.Y.V.E. is hereby detailed for duty in the Qr. Mrs Dept. of this command, and will report immediately to Lieut Templeton A.Q.M.

Special Orders No. 80 City Point Va, Sept 9th. 1864

Lieut J.L. Roosa, 50th N.Y.V.E. will proceed to Washington in charge of Sixteen (16) sick and two (2) attendants. He will turn them over to the Surgeon in charge of the Brigade Hospital at the Engineer Depot Washington

Lieut Roosa having accomplished this and his other business, will return to these Head Quarters.

Special Orders No. 81 City Point Va, Sept 11th 1864

The following named enlisted men belonging to Co "A," 50th N.Y.V.E. being about to be mustered out of service, are hereby directed to proceed to Washington and report to Col W.H. Pettes, Comd'g Engr Depot

Sergt Francis C. Miller	Private John R. Robinson
" W.H. Turner	" Hugh Crescadin
Private Theodore Crescadin	" Asa C. Phelps
" Edwin McMillen	" Edward Lewis

They will join the detachment of their regiment when it leaves Washington for Elmira. Private H. Dean will accompany the detachment to Washington.

I.I. Private Louis Bernkopf Co "A" 15th N.Y.V.E. is hereby detailed for duty as Orderly at these Head Qrs. until further orders, and will report as soon as possible.

Special Orders No. 82, City Point Va, Sept 12th 1864

The following named enlisted men are hereby detailed for duty in the Qr Mrs. Dept of this command, and will report at once to Lieut Geo Templeton A.Q.M.

Private Peter Dendmore Co A, 50th N.Y.V.E.	Priv. Chas Mack Co A,
" Chas Godfier " A " " " " "	15th N.Y.E.
" Abram Reed " B 15th " " " "	" Patrick Cogan " d "
" Hugh McMannis " B " "	" Michael Kenny " D "

I.I. Lieut C.H. Lewis 15th N.Y.V.E. will proceed to Deep Bottom and report to Capt. Lubey for duty. He will remain with Co C until Capt Lubey returns from his leave of absence.

Special Orders No. 83 City Point Va, Sept 13th 1864

Private B.F. Smith Co "A" 50th N.Y.V.E. is hereby detailed for duty at these Head Quarters until further orders.

Special Orders No. 84 City Point Va. Sept 13th 1864

I. during the temporary absence of the General Commanding, Capt Stephen Chester 15th N.Y.V.E. and Brigade Inspect. the senior officer president will be in command of the camp.

II. Lieut F.S. Livingston A.D.C. will proceed to Washington to join his Commanding General, who is to be in Washington on duty.

Special Orders No. 85 City Point Va Sept 15th/64

Corporal Isaac V. Lawrence Co A, 50th N.Y.E. with three men of his regiment is hereby directed to proceed to Engineer Depot Washington D.C. and report to Col W.H. Pettes

The week of September 17 the army's chief engineer reported that over 16 miles of works had by then been built, including 19 forts and re-doubts and 41 batteries. "In addition to the labor on these works, including the obstructions in their front, bombproofs, magazines, and drainage in the interior, nearly 2,000 yards of roads and one-third of the covered ways had been 'corduroyed,' and 6,700 square feet of substantial bridging built. The old intrenched lines were also being leveled. These labors were continued during the following week, the officers and men of the regular battalion of engineers and of the Fiftieth New York Volunteer Engineers having the construction of them."[1]

Special Orders No. 86 City Point Va Sept 19 1864

Lieut R.O'S. Burke 15th N.Y.V.E. at present under arrest is hereby allowed to visit any point within the fortifications of City Point.

Special Orders No. 87 City Point Va Sept 18 1864.

Lieut J. Burden Co A, 50th N.Y.V. Engineers

Sergeant W Dwyer Cp D. 15th N.Y.V.E.	Corpl Joseph Hilbert Co A 15th N.Y.E.
" John Connor " D " " "	" W Hessle " A " "
" James Mahen " A " " "	" Saml Church " D " "&
" Robinson " A " " "	" William Gibson " D " "

are hereby detailed to take charge of the recruits now at this camp. Lieut Burden will report to these Head Quarters for orders. The above Sergeants and Corporals will report immediately to Lieutenant Burden.

Special Orders No 88. City Point Va Sept 20/64

Private Wm Brown Co D, 15th N.Y.V.E. is hereby detailed for duty in the Qr. Mrs. Dept of this command until further orders, and will immediately [report] to Lieut Templeton A.Q.M.

Special Orders No. 89 City Point Va Sept 20 1864.

A General Court Martial is hereby appointed to meet at these Head Qrs tomorrow, Sept 21 at 10 A.M. or as soon thereafter as practicable, for the trial of Private Gilbert McMurtrie Co D 15th N.Y.V.E. and such other prisoners as may be brought before it.

Detail for the Court.

1 Capt Stephen Chester	Brigade Inspector
2 " J. Thomas Elliott	C.S.
3 " H.B. Dribbell,	15th N.Y.V. Engineers
4 Lieut C. Henderson	" " "
5 " Flavious Dibbell	" " "
6 " A.H. Magarer	" " "

Lieut Frank S. Livingston A.D.C. Judge Advocate

No other officers than those named can be assembled without manifest injury to the service.

II. The following named enlisted men are hereby detailed for duty with the G.C.M. and will report immediately to Lieut Livingston A.D.C. & Judge Advocate, for orders

Private D.W. Lee, Co E, 15th N.Y.V.E. as Clerk

" John Jones " A " " " " " Orderly

Special Orders No 90 City Point Va Sept 23 1864

I. Capt H.B. Dibbell 15th N.Y.V.E., a member of the General C.M. now in session at these Head Qrs, is hereby relieved from such duty, and Lieut P.C. Kingsland A.D.C. will act as member of said Court.

General Order No 29 City Point Va Sept 26th 1864

I. Before a General Court Martial of which Capt. Stephen Chester, Brigade Inspector is President convened at Head Qrs Engineer Brigade, City Point Va by virtue of Special Orders No. 89 of Sept 20 1864 from these Head Qrs, were arraigned and tried.

1. Private Timothy Hurley Co C. 15th N.Y.V.E. upon the following

Charge	Drunkenness on Post
Finding	Guilty
Sentence	To be put at hard labor for the period of 30

days with a ball and chain weighing not less than 24 pounds, attached to his left leg, and when not at such hard labor to be placed in confinement.

2 Private Martin Fitzgerald Co. D. 15th N.Y.V.E. upon the following

Charge	Desertion of Post
Finding	Not Guilty

And the Court does therefore acquit him

II. The Records of the General Court Martial in the foregoing cases having been submitted for the action of the General Comdg. Brigade, the following are the orders thereon.

The proceedings findings and sentence in the case of Private Timothy Hurley Co C 15th N.Y.V.E. are approved and the Commanding Officer of the 15th Regt will see that the sentence is carried into effect.

The proceedings and findings in the case of Private Martin Fitzgerald are approved, and he will be released from arrest - and restored to duty

General Order No. 30 City Point Va Oct 1st 1864

I. Before a General Court Martial of which Capt Stephen Chester, Brigade Inspector is President, convened at Head Qrs Engineer Brigade, City Point Va. by virtue of Special Orders No. 89 of Sept 20 1864 from these Head Qrs were arraigned and tried

1st Artificer Henry Jarvis, Co D. 15th N.Y.V.E. upon the following

Charge 1st - Absence without leave
Charge 2nd - Drunkenness
Charge 3rd   Drunkenness on Duty
Finding   Guilty
Sentence   To be reduced to a second class private, to forfeit his monthly pay for the period of six months, to perform all his regular company duties and in addition as far as practicable to make one of every fatigue party detailed from his company during that period.

2nd Private Florentine Bormany Co A. 15th N.Y.V.E. upon the following

Charge   Desertion
Specification In this that he the said Florentine Bormany a private of Co A 15th N.Y.V.E. having been duly enlisted into the service of and received from the United States, did desert the said service, on or about the second day of May 1864 and did absent himself from his company and regiment, without proper authority, remaining so absent until duly arrested and returned to his company and regt under guard. This at Camp of the Engineer Brigade, Engineer Depot - Washington D.C. on or about the second day of May 1865.

Finding. -   Of the charge, Not Guilty, but Guilty of absence without leave.

Of the Specification - Guilty, except the words "and did receive pay from" and of the words "did desert said service, on or about the 2nd day of May 1864."

Sentence.   In addition to the 30 dollars already paid for his apprehension, to forfeit his monthly pay for the period of three months, and during the period of sixty days, in addition to his regular company duties, to form, as far as practicable, one of every fatigue party detailed from his company.

II. The records of the General Court-Martial in the foregoing cases having been submitted for the action of the General Commandg Brigade, the following are the orders thereon.

The proceedings findings, and sentences, in the cases of Artificer Henry Jarvis Co D. and Private Florentine Bormany Co A. 15th N.Y.V.E. are approved and the commanding officer of the 15th Regt will see that the sentences are carried into effect.

General Order No. 31 City Point Va Oct 4th. 1864

I. Before a General Court Martial of which Capt Stephen Chester, Brigade Inspector is President, convened at Head Qrs Engineer Brigade City Point Va. by virtue of Special Order No. 89 of Sept 20 1864 from these Head Qrs were arraigned and tried

1st Private James McLaughlin Co B 15th N.Y.V.E. upon the following

Charge 1st	Sleeping on Post
Charge 2nd	Disobedience of orders
Finding	Guilty
Sentence	To be dishonorably discharged from the ser-

vice of the United States, and to be put at hard labor at the Dry Tortugas, Florida, or such other place as the Commanding General may direct, for the period of three (3) years

2nd Private W.W. Gibson Co D. 15th N.Y.V.E. upon the following

Charge	Sleeping on Post
Finding	Guilty
Sentence	To be dishonorably discharged [from] the

service of the United States, to forfeit all pay, including Bounty, that is or may become due him, and to be put at hard labor at The Dry Tortugas, Florida, or such place as the Commandg Genl may direct, for the re-maining period of his enlistment, expiring April 14th 1867.

3rd Private John McKeever. Co A. 15th N.Y.V.E. upon the following

Charge	Sleeping on his Post
Finding	Guilty
Sentence	To be dismissed [from] the service of the

united States, with forfeiture of all pay that is or may become due him, and afterwards to be put at hard labor at the Dry Tortugas, Florida, or such other place as the Commanding General may direct, for the re-maining period of his enlistment expiring February 14th 1865.

4th Private Peter Coligan Co B 15th N.Y.V.E. upon the following

Charge	Sleeping on Post
Finding	Guilty
Sentence	To forfeit one half his monthly pay for the

period of six months, and during that time to be put at hard labor at such places the Commanding General may direct.

5th Private Henry Muller. Co B. 15th N.Y.V.E. upon the following

Charge 1st	Sleeping on Post
Charge 2nd	Drunkenness on Duty
Finding	Guilty

Sentence   To be put at hard labor at such place as the commanding General may direct, for the period of one year; and to forfeit all pay that may become due him during that period.

II. The proceeding of the General Court Martial in the foregoing cases having been transmitted to the General Convening the Court, the following are the order thereon.

The proceedings findings, and sentences, in the cases of Private James McLaughlin Co B. - William. W. Gibson Co D. John McKeever Co A. Peter Colligan, Co B. and Henry Mullen Co B. 15th N.Y.V. Engrs. are approved. Dry Tortugas is designated as the place of confinement for all the above prisoners.

The prisoners will be turned over to the Provost Marshal General of the Army of the Potomac, with a copy of this order, and their descriptive lists.

On October 4 Benham received help from some professional Army Corps of Engineer officers in creating the line of fortifications around City Point, his overall command. The line, some three miles in all, consisted of eight small redoubts.

On the twentieth officers and men of the 50th voted. Each man was sworn and then received a ballot for the candidate of his choice, Lincoln or McClellan, which he then put into an envelope which was sent to his local town election official.

By October 22 the army's chief engineer was able to report to Major General George G. Meade, Army of the Potomac commanding general, that "the whole line occupied by the Army of the Potomac was entirely constructed and in a defensible condition. Some minor details still required attention. Additional obstacles, palisades, and fraises in connnection with the abatis and wire entanglements had been rapidly pushed forward every night to strengthen it."[2]

General Order No. 32 Defences of City Point Oct 27th. 1864

I. Before a General Court Martial of which Captain Stephen Chester Brigade Inspector, is President, convened at Head Quarters Engineer Brigade, City Point Va. by virtue of Special Orders No. 89 of Sept 20th from these Head Quarters, were arraigned and tried

1. Private Martin Gibson Co E. 15th N.Y.V.E. upon the following
>   Charge   Desertion
>   Finding   Not Guilty

and the court does therefore acquit him

2. Artificer Patrick Quilty of Co "D" 15th N.Y.V.E. upon the following
>   Charge   Conduct to the prejudice of good order and
>   military discipline
>   Finding   Guilty
>   Sentence   To be reduced to a 2nd class Private and to

forfeit his monthly pay for the period of one month

3. Henry A. Coon, Private of Co E. 15th N.Y.V.E. upon the following
  Charge   Desertion
  Finding   Not Guilty
and the court does therefore acquit him
    4 Private John Crawford Co K, 50th N.Y.V.E. upon the following charges.
        Charge 1st.   Desertion
        Charge 2nd.   Conduct to the prejudice of good order and
                  military discipline
        Specification to 2nd charge: In this, that he, said John Crawford private Co K. 50th Regt N.Y.V.E. did in the presence of his superior officer simulate drunkenness, and conduct himself in a disorderly manner, surreptitiously entering upon and concealing himself on board of a steamer about to sail for Washington D.C. and remaining there concealed until discovered and arrested and removed by Lieut John A. Sibbalds 50th N.Y.V.E.
        Finding -   of the 1st Charge   Not Guilty
                  of the Specification of the 2nd charge - Guilty, except where words "simulate drunkenness," and except of the words "upon and concealing himself," and except of the word "concealed."

        of the 2nd Charge   Guilty
        Sentence - To forfeit his monthly pay for the period on one month and during said period, to form as far as practicable, one of every fatigue party detailed from his company -

    II. The proceedings, findings and sentences of the General Court Martial, having been approved by the General Commanding Brigade, the following are the orders thereon.

    The proceedings, findings, and sentences in the cases of Artificer Patrick Quilty 15th N.Y.V.E. & Private John Crawford Co K 50th N.Y.V.E. are approved. The Commanding Officers of the Regiments to which they belong will see that the sentences are carried out.

    The Proceedings and Findings in the cases of Private Martin Gibson Co B. and Private Henry A. Coon Co E. 15th N.Y.V. Engrs. are approved, and they will be returned to duty with the companies to which they belong.

General Order No. 33, Defences of City Point, Oct 28th 1864

    I. Major Trumbull 1st Conn. Heavy Artillery is hereby appointed Chief of Artillery for the defences of City Point and he will be obeyed and respected accordingly.

    I.I. Col J.A. Mathews Commander of the Post at Old Court House is especially charged with the supervision of all pickets in his front, both of cavalry and infantry, and with the command of all troops in rear of the defences of the lines on the left or South of the Rl. Rd.

    I.I.I Lieut Col J.F. Walcott 61st Mass is hereby placed in charge of the troops in rear of the defenses of the lines on the right or North of the Rl. Rd. The senior officer of the Battalion of the 18th New Hampshire will report to him for orders and take his direction in any emergency. Lieut-Col. Pierce chief Quarter Master of the army trains is desired to direct the commanders of the two provisional battalions of the Qr. Mrs Dept. nearest to Col. Walcotts camp to put themselves in communication with Col. Walcott to take his directions in any such emergency.

IV. Commanding Officers of Regiments and Detachments in this Brigade will muster their men for pay on the 31st inst.

Benham's command at City Point in the fall grew to include non-engineers needed for the defense of this active post in a combat area.

General Order No. 34 Defences City Point Oct 30 1864

In compliance with orders from Headquarters of the Army Commanding Officers of Regiments and Detachments in this command will have an inspection of their men at the earliest practicable moment and see that they are all provided with Knapsacks also with Canteens, Haversacks, and overcoats.

On November 7 the army's chief engineer was directed "to furnish General Benham, commanding defenses of City Point, with the project of the line of intrenchments from Prince George Court-House to Old Court-House and also to indicate what was necessary to be done to connect the right of that line with the rear intrenchments resting on the Blackwater."[3]

General Order No. 35 Defences of City Point Dec 28th 1864

Commanding officers of Regiments and Detachments in that command will muster their men or pay on the 31st inst.

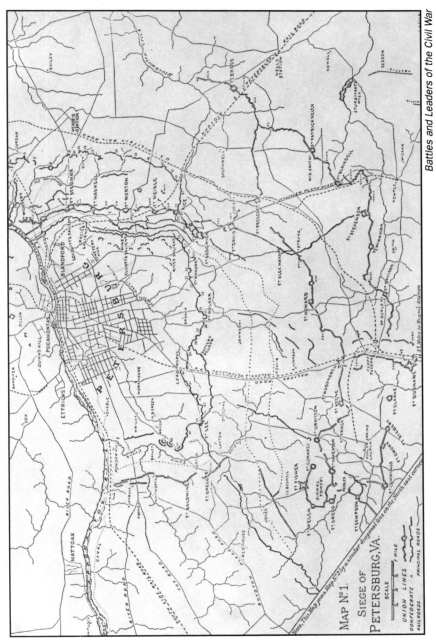

MAP Nº 1.
SIEGE OF
PETERSBURG, VA.

SCALE
½   ¼   1 MILE
——— UNION LINES
------ CONFEDERATE "
—— RAILROADS   PRINCIPAL ROADS

Note.—This Map joins Map Nº 2 by a similar diagonal line on the North east corner

Battles and Leaders of the Civil War

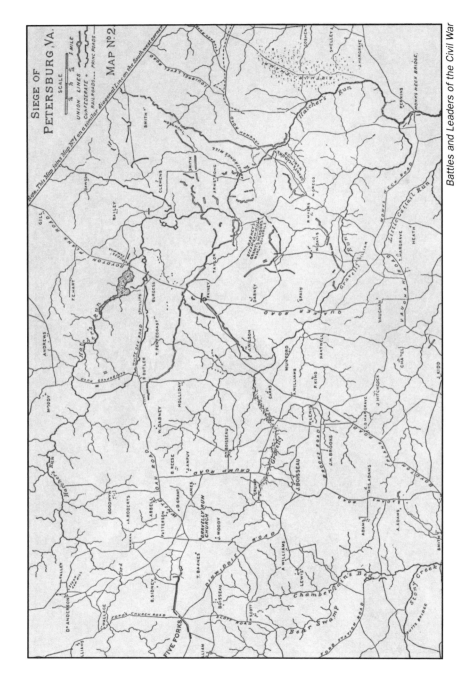

SIEGE OF
PETERSBURG, VA.

MAP Nº2

SCALE
½ ¼ ¾ 1 MILE

UNION LINES
CONFEDERATE "
RAILROADS
PRINC. ROADS

Note. This Map joins Map Nº1 on a similar diagonal line on the South west corner.

Battles and Leaders of the Civil War

CHAPTER 7
The End: 1865

▶————————◀

General Orders No. 1 Defences of City Point Jan'y 6th 1865

I. Before a General Court Martial of which Major S. Sergant 15th N.Y.V.E. is President, convened at Head Quarters Engineer Brigade, City Point Va. by virtue of Special Orders No. 121 of Dec 25th 1864, from these Head Quarters were arraigned and tried.

1 John Fagan, Artificer, Co D, 15th N.Y.V.E. upon the following

Charge	Conduct to the prejudice of good order and Military Discipline
Finding	Guilty
Sentence	To be reduced to Private and in addition to

forfeit his monthly pay for the period of three (3) months.

2 Francis L. McCarthy, Co A, 15th N.Y.V.E. upon the following

Charge	Conduct to the prejudice of good order and Military Discipline
Finding	Guilty
Sentence	To forfeit three months pay, and to be pa-

raded in front of the Brigade Guard House each day for, twenty successive days from Guard Mount to Retreat, wearing a placard marked in large letters "Impostor" and a knapsack weighing not less than thirty (30) pounds.

3. Thomas Duffy, Private Co "E." 61st Mass. Vols. upon the following

Charge	Conduct prejudicial to good order and military Discipline
Finding	Guilty

General Orders No 2 City Point Jan'y 9th. 1865

I. 1st. Lieut John L. Roosa Co G, 50th Regiment N.Y.V. Engrs is hereby relieved from duty as ambulance officer in order to be mustered out of service. He will turn over all Quarter Master property, Camp & Garrison Equipage in his possession to his successor:

I.I. 1st Lt. George T. Dudley Co M. 50th N.Y.V.E. is hereby appointed ambulance officer of the Engineer Brigade and will be respected & obeyed accordingly.

Before an officer could be mustered out of service, the adjutant general's department had to report "to the War Department the state of such officer's accounts of money, as well as of public property, for which he may have been responsible."

General Orders No. 3 City Point Va. January 14th 1865

I. Brigade Guard mounting will be discontinued until further orders.

I.I. The guard for this encampment will be mounted daily at 8 A.M. in the manner prescribed for Regimental guards - the Detachment 50th Regt. furnishing daily 9 enlisted men & one non-commissioned officer for these duties as heretofore.

General Orders No. 4 City Point January 20th 1865

I. Before a General Court Martial of which Major Sewall Sergant 15th Reg. N.Y.V. Eng's is President, convened at H'd Qtr's Eng. Brigade, City Point, by virtue of special Orders No. 121 of Dec 25th. 1864, from these Head Quarters, was arraigned and tried.

Cyril C. Lyon, private of Co K. 15th. Regt N.Y.V. Eng's upon the following

Charges - Conduct prejudicial to good order & military discipline

Findings. Guilty

Sentence - To be dishonorably discharged the Service of the United States, and to be put at hard labor for the remaining portion of his enlistment expiring on the Sixth day of September 1865, without pay, on such Government works as the proper authorities may designate

II. The records of the proceedings of the above Gen'l Court Martial, having been transmitted to the Brig' Gen'l Commanding, the following are the orders thereon.

The above Sentence is too severe for the crime as proved particularly on taking into consideration the address of the envelope, and the note which might have deceived a well meaning man. The principal wrong done, being the Signature to the receipt, to the Express Office. - After the other error - a temptation resulting from the note of information, and the address of the envelope.

In consequence therefore of these doubts, and the testimony as to good character, the Sentence is remitted, except as to the forfeiture of the whole of his pay during the balance of his term of enlistment which will be enforced

General Orders No. 5 City Point, January 21st. 1865

I During the temporary absence of Brig' Gen'l H.W. Benham, on duty, under orders from the Major General Commanding the Army; the next Senior Officer of this command present - Colonel Wesley Brainard, 15th Regiment, New York Engineers, will in addition to the command of his own regiment, be charged with the command of the troops, assigned to the Defences of City Point, and he will be respected and obeyed accordingly.

General Orders No. 6 Defences of City Point Feb 20/65

The General Commanding directs that in compliance, with the request of the Provost Marshal General, no men belonging to this command will be allowed the interior line of Defences of City Point, without a pass from the Comd'g officer of the Detachment to which they belong, countersigned at these Head Qrs. any men about the Point without such passes will be liable to arrest by the Provost-Guard, and imprisonment in the "Bull Ring."

General Orders No. 7 Defences of City Point Feb'y 21, 1865

Complaints having been made that mounted Officers insist upon entering the Forts without dismounting it is hereby ordered, that no Officer shall be allowed inside the works, mounted, except the General Comd'g & his Staff, General Officers, Superior to him in rank, the Colonel of the 15th N.Y. Engineers, and the Engineer Officer in charge of the works.

No animals of any kind will be allowed inside the works except when absolutely necessary for the performance of some duty.

General Orders No. 8 Defences City Point, March 10th 1865

1st Lieut C.M. Bromley 15th N.Y.V. Engineers is hereby appointed acting assistant quarter master of this command and will be obeyed and respected as such accordingly.

General Orders No. 9 Defences City Point, March 14th 1863 [sic]

There will be a Review of the troops of this command to-morrow at 2 P.M. on the ground between the camp of the 18th. N.H. Vols. and the Head Quarters of the 15th. Engineers. The troops will report on the ground at 1 1/2 P.M. when a Staff Officer will be present to assign them their positions in line.

The men will have their canteens, haversacks, woolen & Rubber blankets and knapsacks.

General Orders No. 10 Defences City Point, March 15th/65

Comd'g Officers of Regiments & Detachments of this command will immediately cause requisitions to be forwarded for a sufficient number of knapsacks, haversacks, canteens, woolen & Rubber blankets to equip every man of the command.

Obviously, the review disclosed that some troops were missing important equipment such as their blankets, ponchos, canteens, knapsacks, and haversacks.

General Orders No. 11 Defences of City Point, March 19th 1865

The change of troops in the Defences necessitated a change in the position of the Field officers and until further orders Lieut-Col. Ketchum will remain in general charge of the Forts on the line north of the Railroad. Major Henderson will take post at Fort Porter and take charge of the Forts South of the Railroad. Major Sergant will take charge of the picket-line, each part of which he will inspect & instruct as far as needed daily.

Lieut Burke will continue in charge of the working parties for the completion and repair of the works, and as many men will be furnished daily for fatigue as can be spared from picket, guard duty &c.

General Orders No. 12 Defences City Point, March 28th 1865

I. Before a General Court Martial of which Col. C.F. Walcott 61st Mass. Vols is president, convened at these Head Qrs, by virtue of Special Orders no. 21 of March 6th. 1865, from Hd. Qrs. Engineer Brigade, and Defences City Point, were arraigned and tried

1. Private John Sheehan, Co A, 15th N.Y.V. Engrs. upon the following.

Charge	Desertion
Findings	Guilty
Sentence	To forfeit all pay and allowances now due him

to make good the time lost by his desertion, and to forfeit ($5.00) five dollars of his monthly pay for the period of (15) fifteen months.

2. Private Joseph Seifts, Co. E. 15th N.Y.V. Engrs. upon the following

Charge	Absence without leave
Findings	Guilty
Sentence	To make good the time lost by his absence

without leave, to forfeit all pay and allowances due him for that time, and to be confined under guard for (30) thirty days at hard labor at such place as the Command'g General may direct.

3. Act. 1st. Sergt. P.S. Wickham Co. F. 15th N.Y.V.E. upon the following charges

Charge 1st. Using disrespectful language to his superior officer

Specifications 1st. In this, that he the said Act 1st. Sergeant P.S. Wickham Co F, 15th N.Y.V. Engineers, being ordered under arrest by his superior officer 1st. Lt. N.E. Linsley did say to the said Lieut Linsley in a defiant contemptuous manner, "All right - there's a day coming yet," or words to that effect, which words he the said Act 1st. Sergt. P.S. Wickham repeated three or four times

This at Camp at Fort Merriam, Defences City Point Va. on or about the 12th day of March 1865

Charge 2nd. Disobedience of Orders

Charge 3rd. Conduct prejudicial to good order & military discipline

Specification - In this that he the said Act 1st Sergt. P.S. Wickham of Co F. 15th N.Y.V. Engrs. did in the presence of the enlisted men of the company, conduct himself in a very defiant and contemptuous manner, towards his superior officer, 1st Lieut N.E. Linsley of said Regiment.

This at Camp at Fort Merriam, Defences of City Point Va. on or about the 12th day of March 1865.

Findings.

Of the 1st Specification of Charge 1st "Guilty" except as to the words "repeated " three or four times"

Of the 2nd Specification of Charge 1st.   "Not Guilty"

Of the 1st Charge   "Guilty"

Of the 2nd Charge   "Guilty"

Of the Specification of Charge 3rd "Guilty" except as to the word "very"

Of the 3rd Charge   Guilty

Sentence   To do duty in the ranks for one month as a private, uniformed and paid as such; to ask pardon of the Officer offended, 1st Lieut N.E. Linsley in the presence of Co F. 15th N.Y.V.E. and at the end of the month to be restored to his position as Sergeant, if the Commanding Officer of his regiment shall approve thereof.

4. Private Alexander Parquet, Co E, 1st Maine S.S. upon the following
Charge   Desertion
Finding   Not Guilty
And the Court does therefore acquit him

5. Private Landon C. Buzzel Co. C. 18th N. Hamps. Vol. upon the following
Charge   Drunkenness on duty
Finding   "Guilty"
Sentence   To be confined at hard labor for (30) thirty days at Head Qrs. of his regiment (10) ten days of which time to stand on a barrel from 7 A.M. to 6 P.M. of each day, with one hours intermission at noon, having on his back a placard labeled "Drunk on Duty.

II. The records of the General Court Martial in the foregoing cases having been submitted to the General Commanding Brigade, the following are the orders thereon.

The proceedings findings & sentences in the cases of Private John Sheehan Co "A" 15th and Act. 1st Sergt. P.S. Wickham, Co. F, both of the 15th N.Y.V.E. and Private London C. Buzzell, Co C, 180th N. Hamp. Vol. are approved and the Comd'g officers of the regiments to which they respectively belong will see that their sentences are carried into effect.

In the case of Private Joseph Seifts Co. E, 15th N.Y.V.E. the proceedings, findings & sentence are approved, but in accordance with the unanimous recommendation of the Court that part of the sentence "to be confined for 30 days at hard labor" is remitted.

The proceedings and findings in the case of Private Alexander Parquett, Co C, 1st Maine S[harp].S[hooters]. are approved. He will accordingly be restored to duty.

On March 29 an attack on the Confederate works all along the line was ordered. The sharpest fighting took place along the Union left.

General Orders No. 13 Defences City Point, March 30th. 1865

The troops of this command and of the Garrison of this post, when acting in conjunction with them, on the Defensive lines of City Point, in emergencies, or in expectations of an attack (though available for defence wherever required) will habitually be stationed as follows

The 68th Pa. Regt. Col. Tippen, - between Forts Abbott and Craig, but near Fort Craig, on the north of Telegraph road. The 61st Mass Col. Walcott, at Fort Graves, South of, and near Telegraph road. The 114th Pa. Major Bowen, next North of, and adjacent to Fort Lewis O. Morris, near the Railroad. The 20th N.Y. Col Carderburgh, between Forts Merriam and Gould, South of bridge, just South of Rail Road, South of and near the graveyard of 50th N.Y. Engineers. The Dismounted Cavalry will be stationed just north of the 2nd Maine Battery near Fort Porter. The 15th N.Y. Engineers, will picket Baileys creek and in front as present, and garrison the different Forts, being aided, in the latter duty if required, by a portion of dismounted cavalry.

The Artillery under Capt. Mayo of the Batteries, assisted by Capt. Gilbert of the Siege Artillery, will man the cannon in the Fortifications as at present.

The Cavalry will perform the scouting and patrol duty required in front of the pickets on Baileys Creek, from Prince George C.H. to the James River, and the vidette duty in front or West of the main line.

The infantry regiments above designated being of the Brigade of Brevet Brig. Genl. Collis, will continue under his special command, he being the second in command on the line. The garrison of the Forts, consisting of the Engineer troops, and dismounted cavalry, will form a provisional brigade , under Col. Wesley Brainerd (he still retaining command of the 15th Engrs.) and the portion not needed as garrison will perform the picket duty ordered on the lines and be available for the defence within wherever required.

The mounted force, while on this duty being occupied beyond and for the protection of the whole line of defence, will necessarily receive their instructions from these Head Quarters.

By April 2 the Confederates were no longer able to hold their lines around Petersburg at most parts and began pulling out. The Federals moved across what had been no-man's land to occupy the works so well defended by their enemy.

General Orders No. 14 Defences of City Point, April 4th. 1865

The Commanding General has the pleasure of forwarding to the different portions of the command engaged in the defence of City Point the accompanying testimony of the approbation of Major General Parke, Commanding 9th. Army Corps, for their prompt and efficient performance of duty in supporting him during the recent operations which resulted in the Capture of Petersburg.

And while the Commanding General is much gratified with the promptness of the 15th Regiment of Engineers, gathered as it was from the several Forts which it had occupied on the 2nd inst., and the readiness with which it met the calls upon it for support during that day & night, he has especial pleasure in acknowledging the rapidity with which the several Infantry regiments, the 114 Penna., the 68th. Pa., the 20th. N.Y. and the 61st. Mass, moved forward from these lines to the front, under the direction of their respective commanding officers, and by which promptness only they were enabled to come into action at the most crucial moment and secure as it evidently appeared the works captured from the enemy on the previous night, from a recapture, with great slaughter to the gallant troops who had previously taken and held these lines of the enemy.

Federal troops headed out after Lee, who was trying to go west and then south to join the Army of Tennessee under General Joseph Johnston in North Carolina. Confederate W.W. Blackford, lieutenant colonel of the 1st Regiment of Engineer Troops, the opposite number in the opposing army, remembered that, "During the retreat our regiment formed the rear guard on the road we traveled, breaking up the bridges as we passed and constructing new ones as much as possible in the advance."[1]

Federal engineers headed out with the army, laying down bridges across rivers as Confederate engineers destroyed the ones they had laid before them. "I always found a night march with the Engineer Corps quite an exciting experience," wrote artist and correspondent Edwin Forbes. "The enemy's rear guard seemed to find a malicious—though perhaps natural—pleasure in placing all manner of obstacles in the way of the Union advance. Trees were felled across the roads and impassable labyrinths of interwoven boughs would have to be cleared by the engineers' axes."[2]

On April 9 Lee, his army cut off and surrounded by vastly superior forces, surrendered his hungry troops. Fighting for the Volunteer Engineer Brigade was over. Benham's brigade headquarters moved to a camp west of Petersburg and slightly to the south and east of Farmville.

General Orders No. 15 Burkesville Va. April 15th. 1865

The Brigadier General Commanding the Engineer Brigade on reassuming as directed by the Commd'g Genl Army of the Potomac, the command of all the Engineer troops of that army, hereby directs that while the Battalion of Engineer troops are brigaded together and with the Head Quarters, the usual routine duties of camp shall be performed, whenever practicable, at the hours stated below, until otherwise ordered. The calls for which will be notified by a bugle from the Brigade

Band, the Leader of which is charged with, and held responsible for the regularity and accuracy of those calls, for any omission of which he will be held strictly accountable.

Reveille	5.15 A.M.	Breakfast	6. A.M.
Surgeons Call	6.30" "	Fatigue	7.30 " "
Dinner	12 M	Dress Parade	5 P.M.
Guard Mounting	5.45 P.M.	Supper	6 " "
Retreat	Sunset	Tattoo	7.30 " "
		Taps	9 P.M.

Battalion drill when troops are available 2 to 4 P.M. by regiment at call only.

On April 20, Owen, then with his company back at City Point, wrote home:

> There is a report in circulation that the regiment is going overland to Washington. Yesterday, they sent us an invitation to come out to (Burkeville) where they are and make the march with them. 'Very fine thing.' The men of the captain's detachment have only marched between 7 and 800 miles since 27th February and those of my detachment about 500 miles in the same time, and now spread eagles [colonels, marked by the spread eagle badges in their shoulder straps] at headquarters want us to come up and go with them on a pleasure excursion. I can call it nothing else because there is no enemy to chase or chase us and the idea of marching a couple of hundred miles just for the novelty of the thing is 'played.' ["Played out" was a common slang phrase meaning of no merit.][3]

General Orders No. 16, Burkesville Va April 22nd 1865

I. Before a General Court Martial of which Col. C.F. Walcott, 61st Mass. Vol. was president, convened at these Hd. Qrs. (at City Point Va.) by virtue of Special Orders No. 21 of March 6th. 1865, from Hd. Qrs. Engineer Brigade & Defences of City Point, were arraigned and tried.

1. John Rogers, Priv. Co. D. 1st Maine S.S. upon the following

Charge	Desertion
Finding	Of the Specification - Guilty of Absence without leave.
	Of the charge - Not Guilty of Desertion, but Guilty of absence without leave.

Sentence - To be placed in confinement at hard labor for three months, at such place as the Commanding General may direct.

2. John Jenkins Private Co B, 15th N.Y.V.E. upon the following

Charge	Desertion
Finding	Guilty
Sentence	To forfeit all pay and allowances now due him,

to make good the time lost by his desertion, and to be confined for (3) three months at hard labor at such place as the Commanding General may direct.

3. Wm. Sheehan Private Co A, 15th N.Y.V.E. upon the following
    Charge   Desertion
    Finding   Guilty
    Sentence -   To forfeit all pay and allowances now due, to
make good the time lost by desertion, and to be confined for three (3)
months at hard labor at such place as the Commanding General may
direct.

4. Thomas Finley, Private Co B, 15th N.Y.V.E. upon the following
    Charge   Desertion
    Finding   Guilty
    Sentence - To forfeit all pay and allowances now due him,
to make good the time lost by his desertion, and to be confined for
three (3) months, at hard labor at such place as the Commanding General may direct.

II. The records of the General Court Martial in the foregoing cases
having been submitted to the General Commanding Brigade, and to the
Major General Commanding the Army, the following are the orders
thereon.

The proceedings, findings and sentences in the cases of Private
John Rogers, Co. D, 1st Maine S.S. & Privates John Jenkins Co B, Wm
Sheehan Co A, and Thomas Finley Co B, all of the 15th Regt. N.Y.V.E. are
approved, and the Commanding Officers of the regiments to which they
respectively belong will see that their sentences are put into effect, the
privates named being confined and labor performed under regimental
guard.

General Orders No. 17, Manchester Va. May 5th 1865

Col. W. Brainerd 15th N.Y. Engineers will march the two regiments
of Volunteers of the Engineer Brigade by the routes which shall be directed from Head Quarters of the Army of the Potomac, at the head of
the column of that army now moving to Alexandria, repairing roads
and laying such bridges as may be required. On reaching that point
unless otherwise ordered from Hd. Qrs. A-o-P or other superior authority, Col Brainerd will march the command and report to the Head Quarters of the Brigade at Engineer Depot of the Army of the Potomac, near
the Navy Yard at Washington D.C.

The battalion of United States Engineers, now under orders from
Head Quarters of the Army of the Potomac, as soon as relieved from
such duty will be marched by its commanding officer to quarters in the
Engineer Barracks at the Depot at Washington.

General Orders No. 18 Near Fort Berry Va., June 6th 1865

Commandants of Companies about to be mustered out of the U.S.
service whose men are armed with the 'English Sapper Rifle", of the two
feet barrel, will immediately exchange said arms & equipments, with
the Commanding Officer of the U.S. Engineers, who will turn over the
arms he now has in equal numbers to the said commandants.

Companies E, F, G, H, I, K, L, and M, 15th New York Volunteer Engineer Regiment, were mustered out in Washington June 13, 1865. Company C was mustered out there June 14, while Companies A, B, and D were mustered out there July 2. The entire 50th New York Volunteer Engineer Regiment was mustered out in Washington June 13. Edwin Forbes summed up their contributions: "These men were seldom idle; in winter camp or summer march there was always something for their well-trained heads and skilled hands to do. Their loss of life was not as great as in other branches of the service; but they were exposed to much hardship and frequent peril; they did a very noble and indispensable duty, and no army could avail much without their assistance."[4]

Notes

Chapter 1

1. Scott, H.L., *Military Dictionary* (New York, 1864), pp. 256–257.
2. Scott, ibid., p. 257.
3. Official, *Revised Regulations for the Army of the United States 1861* (Philadelphia, 1862), pp. 10–11.
4. Billings, John D., *Hardtack and Coffee* (Glendale, New York, 1970), p. 378.
5. Corbin, Henry C. and Raphael P. Thian, *Legislative History of the General Staff of the Army of the United States* (Washington, 1901), p. 508.
6. Corbin, Henry C. and Raphael P. Thian, ibid., p. 509.
7. *The War of the Rebellion: A Compilation of the Official Records of the Union and Confederate Armies* (hereafter *ORs*), Series III, Vol. II (Washington, D.C., 1881), pp. 279–280.
8. *ORs*, Series I, Vol. V, p. 24.
9. Author's collection, dated August 27, 1861.
10. Dale E. Floyd, *"Dear Friends at Home..."* (Washington, D.C., 1985), p. 25.
11. *ORs*, op. cit., Series III, Vol. II, p. 705.
12. *ORs*, op. cit., Series I, Vol. V, p. 24.
13. Gross, Warren Lee, *Recollections of a Private* (New York, 1890), pp. 19–20.
14. Forbes, Edwin, *Thirty Years After: An Artist's Memoir of the Civil War* (Baton Rouge, La., 1993), p. 14.
15. Billings, John D., op. cit., pp. 378–379.
16. Forbes, Edwin, op. cit., p. 14.
17. Billings, John D., op. cit., pp. 380–381.
18. Billings, John D., ibid., p. 380.
19. *ORs*, op. cit., p. 25.
20. *ORs*, Series I, Series I, Vol. XI, p. 126.
21. *ORs*, Series I, Vol. XI, p. 108.
22. *ORs*, op. cit., p. 126.
23. *ORs,* op. cit., p. 128.
24. Robert Johnson and Clarence Buel, eds, *Battles and Leaders of the Civil War* (New York, 1956), Vol. III, p. 121.
25. Hunt, O.E., "Engineer Corps of the Federal Army," in Miller, Francis, ed., *Photographic History of the Civil War* (New York, 1909), Vol. 5, p. 226.
26. *ORs*, Series I, Vol. XXV, Part I, p. 215.

Chapter 2

1. *ORs*, Series I, Vol. XXIX, Part 1, pp. 226, 677.
2. Billings, John D., op. cit., p. 393.
3. Official, *Revised Army Regulations, 1861* (Philadelphia, 1863), pp. 46–48.
4. Op. cit., *Army Regulations*, p. 514.
5. Billings, John D., op. cit.., p. 378.
6. Floyd, Dale E., ed., *"Dear Friends at home..."* (Washington, 1985), p. 19.
7. Op. cit., *Army Regulations*, p. 71.
8. Op. cit., *Army Regulations*, p. 32.
9. Scott, Colonel H.L., *Military Dictionary* (New York, 1864), p. 21.
10. Scott, Colonel H.L., ibid., p. 14.

Chapter 3

1. Official, op. cit., *Army Regulations,* p. 63.
2. *ORs*, Series I, Vol. XXXIII, p. 450.
3. Floyd, Dale, op. cit., p. 15.
4. Floyd, Dale, op. cit., p. 25.
5. Floyd, Dale, op. cit., p. 28.
6. *ORs*, op. cit., p. 753.
7. Floyd, Dale, op. cit., p. 34.
8. *ORs*, op. cit., p. 982.
9. Floyd, Dale, op. cit., p. 37.

Chapter 4

1. *ORs*, Series I, Vol. XXXVI, Part 2, p. 323.
2. *ORs*, Series I, Vol. XXXVI, Part 2, p. 339.
3. *ORs*, series I, Vol. XXXVI, Part 2, p. 374.
4. Floyd, Dale, op. cit., p. 38.
5. Matter, William D., *If It Takes All Summer* (Chapel Hill, N.C., 1988), p. 13.
6. *ORs*, Series I, Vol. XXXVI, Part 2, p. 563.
7. *ORs,* Series I, Vol. XXXVI, Part 2, p. 598.
8. *ORs*, Series I, Vol. XXXVI, Part 2, pp. 633–634.
9. *ORs*, Series I, Vol. XXXVI, Part 2, pp. 684–685.
10. Lord, Francis, *Civil War Sutlers And Their Wares* (New York, 1969), p. 106.
11. Longacre, Edward G., ed., *From Antietam To Fort Fisher* (Rutherford, New Jersey, 1985), p. 114.
12. Drickamer, Lee C., and Karen D. Drickamer, eds., *Fort Lyon To Harper's Ferry* (Shippensburg, Pa., 1987), p. 78.
13. Drickamer, Lee C., ibid., p. 109.
14. *ORs,* Series I, Vol. XXXVI, Part 2, pp. 733–735.
15. *ORs*, Series I, Vol. XXXVI, Part 2, p. 735.
16. *ORs,* Series I, Vol. XXXVI, Part 2, pp. 852–853.
17. *ORs*, Series I, Vol. XXXVI, Part 3, p. 232.
18. Owen, Thomas, *Dear Friends At Home* (Washington,1985), p. 25.
19. *ORs*, Series I, Vol. XXXVI, Part 3, p. 67.
20. *ORs*, Series I, Vol. XXXVI, Part 3, p. 116.
21. Burton, Deloss S., "Spotsylvania: Letters From The Field An Eyewitness," *Civil War Times Illustrated* (April, 1983), p. 25.
22. Trudeau, Noah Andre, *Bloody Roads South* (New York, 1989), p. 230.
23. Burton, Deloss S., op. cit.., pp. 25–26.
24. *ORs*, Series I, Vol. XXXVI, Part 3, p. 232.
25. *ORs*, Series I, Vol. XXXVI, Part 3, p. 275.
26. *ORs*, Series I, Vol. XXXVI, Part 3, p. 633.
27. Burton, Deloss S., op. cit., pp. 26–27.

28. Floyd, Dale, op. cit., p. 43.
29. *ORs*, Series I, Vol. XXXVI, Part 3, p. 416.
30. *ORs*, Series I, Vol. XXXVI, Part 3, p. 472.

Chapter 5

1. *ORs*, Series I, Vol. XXXVI, Part 3, p. 704.
2. Floyd, Dale, op. cit.., p. 27.
3. Burton, Deloss, op. cit., p. 27.
4. *ORs*, Series I, Vol. XXXVI, Part 3, pp. 717–718.
5. *ORs*, Series I, Vol. XXXVI, Part 3, p. 740.
6. *ORs*, Series I, Vol. XXXVI, Part 3, p. 772.
7. *ORs*, Series I, Vol. XL, Part 1, pp. 210–211.
8. *ORs*, Series I, Vol. XXXVI, Part 3, p. 777.
9. *ORs*, Series I, Vol. XL, Part 1, p. 299.
10. *ORs*, Series I, Vol. XL, Part 1, p. 299.
11. Hunt, O.E., "Engineer Corps of the Federal Army," in Miller, Francis, ed., *Photographic History of the Civil War* (New York, 1909), Vol. 5, p. 248.
12. Blackford, W.W., *War Years with Jeb Stuart* (New York, 1945), p. 262.
13. Floyd, Dale, op. cit., p. 45.
14. Floyd, Dale, ibid., p. 45.
15. War Department, *Revised Regulations for the Army of the United States, 1861* (Philadelphia, 1862), p. 49.
16. Floyd, Dale, ibid., p. 46.
17. Angle, Paul M., ed., *Three Years in the Army of the Cumberland* (Milwood, N.Y., 1990), p. 274.
18. Burton, Deloss, op. cit., p. 25.
19. Official, op. cit.., *Revised Army Regulations*, p. 112.

Chapter 6

1. *ORs*, Series III, Vol. V, p. 174.
2. *ORs*, Series III, Vol. V, p. 176.
3. *ORs*, Series III, Vol. V, p. 177.

Chapter 7

1. Blackford, W.W., *War Years with Jeb Stuart* (New York, 1945), p. 284.
2. Forbes, Edwin, op. cit., p. 14.
3. Floyd, Dale E., op. cit.., p. 85.
4. Forbes, Edwin, op. cit., p. 14.

Index

122